LOVING
THE CHURCH
▲ ▲ ▲
BLESSING THE
NATIONS

Pursuing The Role
Of Local Churches In
Global Mission

GEORGE

Loving the Church . . . Blessing the Nations

Pursuing the Role of Local Churches in Global Mission

George Miley

Authentic

Authentic Media
We welcome your comments and questions.
129 Mobilization Drive, Waynesboro, GA 30830 USA authentic@stl.org
and 9 Holdom Avenue, Bletchley, Milton Keynes, Bucks, MK1 1QR, UK
www.authenticbooks.com

If you would like a copy of our current catalog, contact us at:
1-8MORE-BOOKS
ordersusa@stl.org

Loving the Church . . . Blessing the Nations
ISBN: 1-884543-75-8

Published in 2003 by Authentic Media

Cover design: Paul Lewis
Interior design: Angela Duerksen

Printed in the United States of America

I am delighted with this courageous and balanced book, which helps us toward a more biblical concept of local churches and missions for the twenty-first century.

Patrick Johnstone
WEC International
Author of *Operation World*

Here is a biblical, cutting-edge book from a person with decades of global experience. It is filled with nuggets of wisdom. I believe it will greatly bless you and your church.

George Verwer
Founder and International
Coordinator
Operation Mobilization

George Miley is a man with a large irenic spirit and an equally large and unflinching commitment to the local church and its place in world evangelization. A relevant topic I found throughout was apostolic ministry. The book places this gift as central to the missional quest. This book is challenging and instructive.

Paul McKaughan
President and CEO
Evangelical Fellowship of Mission
Agencies

George, I got home from church this afternoon and started reading *Loving the Church . . . Blessing the Nations.* I could not put it down! This book is God ordained and God anointed. I have never heard your heart as clearly as it comes out in these pages.

Carl Jenks
Senior Pastor
New Hope Community Church
Rochester, N.Y.

In *Loving the Church . . . Blessing the Nations,* George Miley presents the anointed vision of Antioch Network. I urge you to carefully read this book and then keep it as a resource to which you regularly refer.

Gregory E. Fritz
President
Caleb Project

George Miley loves and honors the local church. He sees the awesome power of Christ's love at work in the church, mobilizing teams of disciples to give birth to church planting movements that transcend cultural boundaries. This book chronicles George's journey of discovery and provides patterns of great value to church leaders.

Dan Davis
Pastors in Covenant
Austin, Tex.

As a lay elder, I have come to know firsthand the loving shepherd's heart of George Miley. God has given George a clear vision of the church and great commission for the twenty-first century. This book should be studied by all who love the church and are committed to her mission and place in the world.

Mark A. Talamini, M.D.
Professor of Surgery
Johns Hopkins University
School of Medicine

I find *Loving the Church . . . Blessing the Nations* rich in theology and missiology. It provides me with a wide perspective on missions and the kind of people God uses for his kingdom. I would like to use it as a mission handbook for crew and staff of the *Logos II*.

Lawrence Tong
Director, *Logos II*
Operation Mobilization Ship
Ministry

I have known George for many years, and this book reflects his life passion. It is a blessing for the church, for the missionaries, and for the nations! It shows step-by-step how the church can regain its privilege of full ownership in world mission.

Fritz Schuler
Director, Operation Mobilization
Germany
Chairman, German Association of
Evangelical Mission Societies

George Miley has uniquely, clearly, and powerfully reminded us of the rightful role of the local church in the completion of world evangelism. Our own church planting initiatives in Central Asia have been greatly enhanced by the perspectives and insights contained in *Loving the Church . . . Blessing the Nations*.

Rev. Gregg Parris
Senior Pastor, Union Chapel
United Methodist Church
Muncie, Ind.

George Miley and Antioch Network are hitting a bull's eye with their missions approach. George draws on years of missions experience to design a simple and easy-to-implement methodology to bridge the gap between the local church and the missions movement. This is the most practical and biblical model I have seen.

David Yates
Former Ironman CEO
Missions Consultant

This is the best, most practical mission book I have ever read! George has lovingly wedded and welded the local church with unreached people groups. This is a super-strategic book in the Adopt-A-People Movement and will measurably hasten the Great Commission into becoming the Great Completion!

Dick Bashta
Director
Adopt-A-People Clearinghouse

George Miley is superbly suited to write about the church and reaching the world with the gospel. His mature passion and rich experience are made available to all in a highly readable format that will inspire the reader. This is a visionary book that will play an important role in reaching the nations.

Randal L. Bremer
Senior Pastor
St. Giles Presbyterian Church
Richmond, Va.

Every pastor wrestles with the question of the church's apostolic calling. We know we have a destiny greater than our local congregation, but how do we fulfill it? This book addresses that question, and then some. It answers the big questions and inspires vision. I wish I could have read this book thirty-five years ago—it would have saved me a lot of heartache.

Floyd McCLung
Senior Pastor, Metro Christian
Fellowship
Kansas City, Mo.
Director, All Nations Leadership
Alliance

Loving the Church . . . Blessing the Nations is a fresh perspective for the twenty-first century church. George has a deep understanding of God's heart. He has a unique gift of balancing deep theological truth with practical suggestions. As our church has partnered with George over the years, the vision articulated here has given direction and focus.

Ben Abell
Leader, Senior Leadership Team
Grace Fellowship Church
Baltimore, Md.

George, you have winsomely invited us into your own journey, your love for Christ, and his commission. This is a book I can give to my leaders. The history of mission, the centrality of corporate prayer, and the faithfulness of Jesus to work through his Church with all her shortcomings were enlightening and faith giving.

Sandy Mason
Senior Pastor
Desert View Bible Church
Scottsdale, Ariz.

This is, beyond any doubt, the best material I've read on the subject of missions and the local church. George's loving approach to and treatment of the subject is so refreshing and encouraging. It is extremely relevant *now* to a large and growing number of churches both in the United States and Latin America.

Ramon Bedwell
Castillo del Rey
Monterrey, Mexico

In a powerful and refreshing way, George Miley has captured the pulse of the Holy Sprit, releasing rich giftedness stored up in local churches all over the world. That release is the answer to the prayer Jesus instructed us to pray when he said, "The harvest is plentiful but the workers are few. Ask the Lord of the harvest, therefore, to send out workers into his harvest field." *Loving the Church . . . Blessing the Nations* is a book to savor and to pass on to friends who want to move with God.

Dave Hicks
President/CEO
Bethany Fellowship International

Hanna

You were born Jewish in Hitler's Germany, escaped the Holocaust as a seven year old, grew up in England where you found your Messiah, met me in Belgium, married me in India, served Christ with me all over the world, and continue to be the joy and inspiration of my life. This book tells our journey together.

Thank you for saying yes!

Contents

Foreword

While Christianity is dichotomized with the syndrome of "to be or not to be" regarding the church and parachurch issue, this book by George Miley comes with tremendous clarity. It balances the centrality of the local church, "the called out people of God," and the unquestionable contribution of mission organizations.

While there are many (some useful and some not so useful) theories and assumptions being written about the local church in mission, George writes very strongly from practices he saw work. Most books go from theories to practice, from abstraction to realities. Some theories work; others ultimately cause disillusionment to many. George speaks from practices he has followed in missions coming forth from the churches. There are original insights in this book on the local church in missions, particularly the need for leadership to be spotted, developed, and released into the work. Only thus will the churches be effective in fulfilling the Great Commission of the Lord Jesus Christ.

I have benefited from George's personal input in my life. He has been a significant influence in getting me to where I am today in spirit, mind, and character, trying to fulfill the Great Commission of the Lord Jesus in my realm. I know in reality that what he says works. George continues to follow what he believes—spotting people with character, training them, and releasing them to be Christian leaders around the world on all continents in an ongoing process. I am grateful to God for such leaders.

And Hanna has been the pillar to keep him going where God wanted him to go!

May God be honored by the outcome of this book in bringing and discipling the nations to Christ. I very strongly recommend that people read and practice its insights.

K. Rajendran, General Secretary
India Missions Association • Chennai, India

*   *   *   *   *   *

Loving the Church . . . Blessing the Nations is a stimulating book—liberating, compelling, challenging. This is a visionary manifesto, clearly born out of passion, experience, and solitude! From the first page to the last, George Miley gives us a rare picture of the high calling of the church and the inclusiveness of the Great Commission of Christ.

As an elder involved in setting the spiritual tone of a missions-minded church, I appreciate the holistic outlook that sheds fresh insight on the focus and ownership of a congregation in regards to missions, something so often longed for but too often out of reach.

As a mission leader, responsible for charting the course of an international, mobile Christian ministry community, I appreciate the call and plea for recognizing the importance of the involvement in "blessing the nations" by the local church at both the leadership and the grassroots level.

As a previous co-worker learning from and working with George Miley many years ago, I am excited about the heartbeat of this book. It is concerned with Christ being glorified, the church discovering and fulfilling her calling, and the individual believer growing in character and gifting for the sake of fulfilling God's task.

This is a book for all who care about the church and her calling, a book for all those who care about "making disciples of every nation," a book for you!

Bernd Gülker, Managing Director
Operation Mobilization Ship Ministry • Mosbach, Germany

Introduction

*B*ooks are best written in solitude. The word that brings enduring value to the human world comes from God, and God speaks in the clarifying and healing silences. In the place of busyness and noise, his voice is forced to compete and is too often unheard. So he waits.

My season of life solitude began in 1984 when I was forty-four years old. I did not choose it—I was not that wise. God chose it for me. He alone knew how much I needed it. The choice he left to me was whether I would enter it with grace and faith or anger and bitterness. I chose the latter. He respected my errant decision and stood aside as I reaped the bitter fruit it brought. Then, as I allowed him, he patiently and gently loved me through to healing and restoration.

In one sense, I have emerged from that season of retreat. In another sense, I can never emerge. Solitude has become my lifeline. I know Jesus waits for me there.

Books are best written in community. My community for *Loving the Church...Blessing the Nations* feels especially broad. It begins with my college and seminary professors and fellow students. I write on the foundation they laid. It moves to my co-workers with Operation Mobilization worldwide but especially in India on the ships *Logos* and *Doulos* and those of us who pioneered together the OM Ships headquarters in Mosbach,

Germany. It extends further to the pastors and missionaries I met and served with on five continents and a hundred countries. They taught me volumes.

The senior pastors and church leaders who have formed Antioch Network obviously hold a very special place in my experience. And without the staff team with whom I serve Christ's Church today, this book would have never found its voice. Lincoln Murdoch, you have assumed leadership of the team and ministry in a way that has freed me with full confidence to concentrate on writing. I owe you a huge debt as a friend and co-worker. Thank you for allowing Jesus to continue forming you into a godly man. And Todd Gee, you are a servant of God with keen spiritual insight, a rich and productive mind, and a passion for Jesus that is contagious. Thank you for all the ways you served him and me in finalizing this project.

Books are best written out of life experience. Whether every book is foundationally autobiographical, I do not know. This one is. The reader will walk with me through decades of my inner journey and development before God. And the process is ongoing. There have been mountaintops of exhilaration and valleys of despair. Out of them I have been, and am being, forged.

"My food," said Jesus, "is to do the will of him who sent me and to finish his work." (John 4:34)

The Church,[1] as God designed her to be, is stunningly beautiful. She is the visible body in whom Christ resides, the fullest manifestation of him on earth until he returns in glory (Eph. 1:22–23). She is a bride-to-be, an exquisitely delightful young woman being prepared by the Father for marriage to his Son (Eph. 5:31–32, Rev. 21:1–2). Churches are magnificent. There must be more of them everywhere!

This book is the pursuit of a fuller understanding of God's design for that to happen.

CHAPTER 1

Our Passions

On March 16, 1987, leaders from seven churches gathered to spend a day together. Our purpose was to explore a vision that was living within us—that our churches would focus on how we might start new churches within a strategically selected unreached people group. Throughout the day we shared our individual journeys, prayed for each other, and learned from one another.

We represented a variety of Christian traditions. Some came from denominational churches and others from independent ones. Some were rooted in one theological stream and others in another. But those were not the issues that day. We discovered compelling common ground in worship, prayer, God's heart for all nations, and a whole set of core convictions. What had brought us together was far more powerful than anything that might separate us. When the day was over, we knew we wanted to meet again. We were unaware of it, but Antioch Network had just been born.

Antioch Network

Antioch Network is an expanding fellowship of local churches that are focusing strategically on extending God's kingdom among unreached peoples. We embrace the biblical imperatives imperfectly articulated in this book, not as accomplishments we claim, but as goals to which we aspire, depending only on God's grace to sinners. This book is Antioch Network's manifesto. Its scope, however, must reach far beyond Antioch Network. The only reason for referring to Antioch Network is to establish that the principles here articulated have not been set forth in an ivory tower disconnected from real life. They are being embraced and lived out, albeit imperfectly, by actual churches and their leaders.

> *This book is intended to be a call to, and affirmation of, churches everywhere.*

This book is intended to be a call to, and affirmation of, churches everywhere. It is a cry from the heart about Christ, his actual presence among the community of believers, and his astonishingly grace-filled intention to bless every nation on earth. It is the blending of many voices, the distillation of what untold numbers of churches have and are experiencing. My first mentor in church life and ministry was a church leader in India—Bakht Singh. His influence has deeply enriched these pages. Remembering him prompts me to gratefully acknowledge that other church leaders in Asia, Latin America, Africa, and Europe have taught me volumes.

And we are still learning. It feels like we are standing at the entrance to a vast treasure chamber filled with dazzling riches with which Christ is gracing his Church. "To him be glory in the church" (Eph. 3:21). "Declare his glory among the nations" (Ps. 96:3).

A Manifesto

Manifesto: A public declaration of motives and intentions—*Webster's New World Dictionary.*

I write for church leaders who want to make a public declaration of motives and intentions: to proclaim what we understand God has called us to be and do, to speak out our convictions, and to call more churches and their leaders to join together in catalyzing and serving a movement, focused on the final frontiers of world evangelization. These passions were originally formalized in August 1996 and revised in January 2003.

We Are Passionate . . .

1. To see the Lamb worshipped among all peoples. The eighteenth century Moravians, originally a Christian community (church) of around six hundred adults in Central Europe, matured into the most significant Protestant missionary movement of their time. They were propelled forward by the conviction that "the Lamb must receive the reward of his suffering." Jesus is worthy of nothing less than to be proclaimed, loved, worshipped, and obeyed in every cultural context. It is the final destination of all human history: "All nations will come and worship before you" (Rev. 15:4).

2. To see the local church be held in high regard. Scripture describes the Church as "the fullness of him who fills everything in every way" (Eph. 1:23) and says, "through the church the manifold wisdom of God should be made known" (Eph. 3:10). This is exalted language. Christ endows churches with an awesome capacity waiting to be developed and released. Soon after the resurrection, churches became bases from which church planting teams were sent out among unevangelized cultures (the Gentiles). Kingdom blessings are delivered through spiritually vibrant, culturally relevant churches that are being reproduced throughout society.

> *Soon after the resurrection, churches became bases from which church planting teams were sent out among unevangelized cultures (the Gentiles).*

3. To see every believer be esteemed as a gifted minister. Christ through the Holy Spirit has generously distributed a dazzling variety of spiritual gifts among God's people (Eph. 4:7–8, 1 Cor. 12:7–11). And with good reason! Establishing God's kingdom among every people on earth is a complex process. It calls forth the spiritual gifts, natural abilities, vocational expertise, and life experiences of every believer. The task is too multi-faceted to be viewed as the exclusive domain of a group of religious professionals, though they are certainly included. They are part of the body too! Every believer is invited to join with the Father in fulfilling his mission on earth and is graced with the capacity to play a significant and deeply fulfilling role.

4. *To see mission rooted in community.* Community is the environment of extended family. It is committed relationships developed over time in the midst of real life, providing nurture, support, accountability, and staying power for the long haul. Most believers will not leave home and move somewhere else to participate in a mission. It is not the Father's calling for them to do so. If their unique contribution to God's global purpose is to be made, it will take place right where they are, in the context of the Christian community of which they are a part—their church. Church is not a series of religious meetings. It is a way of life.

5. *To commit to the pastoral care of those we send.* One fundamental image God uses to identify himself in Scripture is that of a father. His mission on earth can be described as God forming a family for himself from among all peoples. It is unthinkable that he would author approaches to world evangelization that are cavalier about the physical, emotional, and spiritual needs of those he sends. God's purposes are most effectively carried out by people who do so out of a fullness rooted deeply in the resources of Christ and overflowing with worship, thanksgiving, and joy. Mature churches are rich with those competent to care pastorally.

6. *To view godly character as primary.* We live in a compulsive age that tries to hammer us into its image. Voices all around tell us that we should be busy and rushed. We are tempted to elevate ability and take action based on it alone. God is slower. His goal is Christ-likeness in the inner person. Accomplishments, even those done in Jesus' name, that do not come forth from the wellspring of godly character will ultimately implode. Man is looking for better methods. God is looking for purer people. The greatest

need in mission is not more activity (although more activity is certainly called for), but more men and women of godly character.

> *The greatest need in mission is not more activity, but more men and women of godly character.*

7. *To keep prayer central in all we do.* A twenty-four–hour prayer chain that endured one hundred years fueled the Moravian missionary advance. Unreached nations are walled off from the kingdom of God by powerful spiritual forces hostile to Christ and his Church. Only the gracious working of God can tear these walls down, and he has chosen to do this work in response to the faithful, faith-filled prayers of his people. As we mature beyond our illusions of what our means can accomplish and grow in our passion to see the hand of God revealed, our joy in and capacity for prayer will deepen appreciably.

8. *To see churches cultivate God-honoring relationships beyond themselves.* Each church carries awesome potential, but if any church begins to think itself is sufficient and doesn't need the rest of the body, that potential is dampened. Jesus' endowment of gracious strengths does not erase areas of need. As relationships of love and trust are cultivated among the wider body of Christ, strengths can be extended and help received. Churches benefit considerably through ongoing interaction with other churches, mission organizations, and mature leaders who have been entrusted by God with a wider ministry among his people.

9. *To see the body of Christ be united.* Jesus is doing new and beautiful things in uniting his people. Churches are finding one another: denominational churches, independent churches, charismatic churches, non-charismatic churches, etc. We are discovering that the things we share—worship, prayer, love for our neighbor, a passion for God's glory among the nations, and, above all else, Christ—far surpass anything that might differentiate us. Churches and mission organizations are learning to honor one

another. Racial and cultural barriers are crumbling. We are not talking about organizational sameness but spiritual unity created by Jesus' residence among us. "Is Christ divided?" (1 Cor. 1:13). Of course not! Antioch Network is intentionally committed to the scriptural injunction to "Make every effort to keep the unity of the Spirit through the bond of peace" (Eph. 4:3).

A note concerning mission organizations: In our passion to champion a high view of the local church, we must be careful to affirm and honor the God-designed role of mission organizations. (You could also use terms such as parachurch organizations, sodalities, apostolic teams, etc.) Throughout the history of the Church in mission, their contribution has been biblical, unmistakable, and profoundly significant. The vision of Antioch Network was born in a mission organization and owes its foundations to perspectives gained there. We honor the ministries of our brothers and sisters who are called by Jesus to serve him in mission organizations. Churches need mission organizations. Mission organizations need churches. We all need one another!

10. To see mission initiatives be strategically focused. Our God-designed finiteness limits what any one of us can effectively undertake. Therefore, our mission initiatives need to be strategic in order to bring maximum glory to Christ. Traditionally many churches have developed mission commitments without strategic integration. Predominately churches have left the formation of strategy to agencies and have just sent people apart from understanding the

> *Predominately churches have left the formation of strategy to agencies and have just sent people apart from understanding the strategic needs and opportunities in the world.*

strategic needs and opportunities in the world. Responding to opportunities as they come up might seem right at first, but the end result will be a shotgun-like effect to which our people will be less and less able to meaningfully engage. The central questions become "What does it mean to complete God's purpose among all nations?" "What strategic opportunities remain?" "In which one(s) is God calling *our church* to be his channel of blessing?" That is where we focus.

These are our passions. Pastors, business people, church planters, laborers, engineers, students, mothers, administrators, and artists, let's join together in living them out!

---

[1]In this book I have followed Patrick Johnstone's lead in his excellent book *The Church Is Bigger Than You Think* (p. 12). *Church* with a capital *C* refers to (1) all believers of all time, (2) the whole company of the redeemed on earth at the present time, or (3) the whole visible Church on earth including all who call themselves Christian. *Church* with a lowercase *c* is used when I am referring to a local church or congregation of believers.

**All nations will come and worship before you.
(Rev. 15:4)**

*The human heart cries out for personal signifi-
cance. We were created that way. We have a visceral
need for our lives to have meaning. When this need
remains unmet, an almost unbearable soul-destroying
emptiness engulfs us. It fosters compulsivity and
addictions of many kinds.*

*Our Creator is a person of purpose. He is on the
move, carrying out his grace-filled, compassionate
intentions for humanity. He designed us to participate
with him in fulfilling his mission on earth. Herein lies
the ultimate purpose for which each of us individually
was designed and created.*

*God's global purposes are not the sole domain of
"missionaries" or "clergy" or "full-time Christian
workers." No! But that discussion is for later chapters. To be able to make the decisions that will release
our personal, God-ordained role in carrying out
God's global mission, we need to have a working
understanding of a vital question: what is God's
mission on earth?*

CHAPTER 2

Every Nation

W hat precisely is God's mission on earth? We need to know. When we do, we can be about getting it done. We can avoid investing energy and resources in activities that may be well intentioned but inadequately conceptualized. We need to know from Scripture what the mission is. Much has already been written on this subject that is excellent and need not be repeated here. In this chapter, we intend only to pause long enough to establish the final goal on earth toward which God is taking us. Thy kingdom come, on earth! This is the foundation on which we build. This book could not begin anywhere else.

There is more than one way to articulate God's declared purpose on earth, but none is better than the words of Genesis 12 where God records his covenant with Abraham. The culminating result that was to come from their relationship is recorded in verse 3: "All peoples [nations] on earth shall be blessed."

When I was in school, the color of India on the world map in front of the classroom was orange. Pakistan was green, China was yellow, and Nepal was purple. In those days, India to me was a single concept, a country or a nation in the way we use the term *United Nations*.

I went to India when I was twenty-six. My port of entry was the city of Mumbai. Soon I was with others distributing tracks on the streets. We had tracks in English because many of the business and professional people speak English. Marathi is the main language of the state where Mumbai is located, so we had Marathi tracks. Hindi is the national language of India, and many people in Mumbai speak Hindi. We also needed Urdu for when we met Muslim people. There are also many in Mumbai from Kerala down in the south, and they speak Malayalam. Others from time to time would ask if we had tracks in their languages—Tamil, Telegu, Gujarati, Bengali, etc. Wow! India was more complex than I had at first understood. Somehow to represent all this, it seemed we needed more than one color.

Things became even more fascinating. Parsees, Zoroastrians who originally came from Iran before the arrival of Islam, owned the restaurant Seven Heavens where we often ate. We met Brahmins, who were the highest cast among the Hindus. There are tens of millions of them—more than the population of most countries. The Dhobis are one of the scheduled castes or Dalits. They would come, collect our clothes, and take them to the river for washing, beating them on the rocks. India was transitioning in my experience from a single entity to a breathtakingly glorious mosaic of cultural groups.

This is precisely what our English Bibles refer to by the terms *nations* or *peoples* or *Gentiles*. They are all the same word in the original Hebrew and Greek. They describe how God sees the world—as an exquisitely fabulous quilt of cultural groups. India is not one nation but a subcontinent containing many nations or peoples. And it is in these terms that God describes his purpose or mission on earth: to bless all peoples, nations, or cultural groupings.

The Biblical Mandate for Global Mission

God's commitment to this global purpose is repeated in hundreds of passages throughout Scripture. The following references are only representative.

The time of the patriarchs. God established his covenant with Abraham and his descendents (Israel) during the time of the patriarchs. God's ultimate purpose was to make Abraham's people a channel of blessing to all the peoples on earth. The "all nations" dimension of this covenant was reaffirmed with Abraham's son, Isaac, and grandson, Jacob.

Genesis 12:3	Genesis 22:18	Genesis 28:14
Genesis 18:18	Genesis 26:4	

Old Testament historical sections. We notice this pattern in the historical sections of the Old Testament: God repeatedly thrusts his people into redemptive contact with other peoples (the Gentiles).

Genesis 41:57	Ruth 1:16	1 Kings 10:1,6-9
Exodus 9:16	1 Samuel 17:46	Daniel 6:25–28
Exodus 12:38	1 Kings 8:43,60	Jonah 1:1–2
Joshua 4:24		

The book of Psalms. Representing the books of poetry, the book of Psalms contains over one hundred references to the scope of God's intentions being global.

Psalm 2:8	Psalm 57:5,9,11	Psalm 98:1–9
Psalm 9:11	Psalm 66:1–8	Psalm 99:1–3
Psalm 18:49	Psalm 67:1–7	Psalm 105:1
Psalm 22:27–28	Psalm 72:8–11	Psalm 108:1–5
Psalm 45:17	Psalm 77:13–14	Psalm 113:3–4
Psalm 46:10	Psalm 86:9	Psalm 126:2
Psalm 47:1–2,7–9	Psalm 96:1–3,7–10	

The Prophets. In the book of the prophets, we see that they foresaw the time when the ways of God would be known not just by Israel but throughout the whole earth.

Isaiah 2:1–4	Isaiah 42:6,10,12	Isaiah 66:18-19
Isaiah 6:3	Isaiah 45:22	Jeremiah 1:5
Isaiah 9:1–2	Isaiah 49:6	Jeremiah 4:2
Isaiah 11:9–10	Isaiah 52:10	Jeremiah 16:19
Isaiah 12:4–5	Isaiah 54:5	Jeremiah 33:19
Isaiah 18:1–2,7	Isaiah 56:6–7	Jeremiah 46:1-2,13
Isaiah 19:21,24–25	Isaiah 60:1-3	Jeremiah 47:1
Isaiah 25:6–9	Isaiah 61:11	Ezekiel 20:9,14,22,41
Isaiah 42:1	Isaiah 62:1-2	Ezekiel 36:19-23

Daniel 4:1	Micah 5:4	Zechariah 2:11
Hosea 2:23	Habakkuk 2:14	Zechariah 8:22-23
Joel 2:28,32	Zephaniah 3:9	Zechariah 14:9
Micah 4:1-3	Haggai 2:7	Malachi 1:11,14

The Gospels. Although Jesus focused on Israel, his ultimate strategic purpose was that his invitation to life in the kingdom of God be extended to all peoples, both Jews and Gentiles.

Matthew 2:1–2	Mark 11:17	John 4:39–42
Matthew 4:12–16,24–25	Mark 16:15	John 12:20–21
Matthew 8:10–12	Luke 2:28–32	John 12:32
Matthew 12:17–21	Luke 4:24–28	John 17:18,20
Matthew 24:14	Luke 24:44–47	John 20:21
Matthew 28:19	John 3:16–19	

The book of Acts. The fulfillment of this purpose is recorded in the book of Acts. The community of God's redeemed (the Church) now includes anyone who relies on Jesus whether from Israel or any other nation.

Acts 1:8	Acts 9:15–16	Acts 11:19–21
Acts 2:5	Acts 10:1,17,28	Acts 13:46–47
Acts 3:25	Acts 10:34–36	Acts 14:23,27
Acts 8:4,14,25	Acts 11:2–3,18	Acts 15:14–19

The Epistles. These letters that make up much of the New Testament celebrate and describe individuals from every people being embraced in the Church.

Romans 1:5	Romans 15:16–17	Ephesians 3:1
Romans 9:16–17	Romans 15:23–24	Ephesians 3:6
Romans 9:24–26	Romans 16:25–26	Ephesians 3:8
Romans 10:18–21	1 Corinthians 9:21–23	Colossians 1:27
Romans 11:25	Ephesians 3:1,6,8	Colossians 3:8
Romans 15:8–12	2 Timothy 4:17	Colossians 3:14

The book of Revelation pictures the final fulfillment of Genesis 12:3. "After this I looked and there before me was a great multitude that no one could count, from every nation, tribe, people and language, standing before the throne and in front of the Lamb" (Rev. 7:9).

Revelation 5:9–10	Revelation 15:4	Revelation 22:17
Revelation 7:9–10	Revelation 22:2	

God's Mission

God states his mission on the earth in unmistakably clear terms: all nations will be blessed. When you look for it, it is hard to miss. God did not want us to be unclear about this. There is a focus: nations or cultural groups.

The process of carrying out God's mission among all nations has been going on for some time now. We are no longer at the beginning of the process. If we were to allow ourselves to strategize seriously about how we might complete this task, how might our thoughts go?

For starters, what if we had a list of nations that have already been blessed? (A fuller discussion of what it means for a nation to be blessed will be taken up in subsequent chapters.) In that case, we could safely remove these blessed nations from our list of candidates for pioneering kingdom initiation (although crucial kingdom ministry would still need to continue among them). Next, we could focus new energies and resources on nations that have not yet been blessed.

How might we define a nation that has not yet been blessed?

It has always been my ambition to preach the gospel where Christ was not known. (Rom. 15:20)

In Scripture, God uses more than one image to express what he is up to. He tells us he is extending his kingdom, growing a family, and working righteousness in individuals and society as a whole. In each of these pictures, God's activities are global.

We have chosen to work with the wording of Genesis 12:3, "All peoples on earth will be blessed." This terminology is not inherently better than others, but it includes them and seems more helpful for developing effective strategies for mission. Notice how this works: God is extending his kingdom among all peoples on earth or God is growing a family from among all peoples on earth or God is bringing righteousness among all peoples on earth.

When God is at work in a culture, that people is in the process of being blessed. The terms that are used in referring to blessed and yet-to-be-blessed peoples are reached and unreached. Look how far we will advance in global strategy development if we can accurately define them:

All peoples minus all reached peoples leaves all unreached peoples, or the task remaining.

CHAPTER 3

Unreached Peoples

"**A**ll peoples on earth will be blessed" (Gen. 12:3). What an awesome statement about God! Who is he? He is a person whose greatest delight and eternal purpose is to bless—a God of compassion, grace, forgiveness, and reconciliation. Nothing in his character enjoys judgment. For him judgment is the last resort when all offers of blessing have been rejected. God does not choose judgment, men do.

Getting Sight of the Target

When I was seventeen years old, I entered the army. Part of basic infantry training was qualifying in the use of the M-1 rifle. There were three levels of achievement: marksman, sharpshooter, and expert. I wanted very badly to qualify as expert.

We began by firing at stationary targets on an open range. I did well. We then moved to a wooded area where we were to fire at silhouettes, representing enemy solders, that would suddenly pop up. Time and again, I heard the soldiers to my right and left fire. But I hesitated; I could not see the targets!

It turned out that there was a slight bump in the terrain where I had been assigned. It hid the targets from me, especially when I was in a kneeling or prone position. I failed to hit enough targets to qualify as expert. But in the process, I learned a valuable lesson:

it is hard to hit targets you cannot see. The clearer the target, the better your chance to hit it.

> *When forming strategies to complete God's mission on earth, it is crucial to be able to see our targets.*

If God's purpose on earth is that "all nations on earth shall be blessed," then it triggers some further questions. These are worthy of careful consideration and precise definitions.

What Is a People (or Nation)?

people: a group of individuals; i.e., the people of London.

a people: a people group (a cultural concept); i.e., the Navajo people (nation).

country: a political, geographical entity (a geographical concept); i.e., the country of India.

nation (popular usage): a country; i.e., The United Nations. The concept of *country* as a geopolitical unit did not fully develop until the dawn of the modern era in fifteenth century Europe with countries like England, France, and Spain. Throughout most of history, including biblical times, there were first peoples (Gen. 11), then empires (Dan. 6:25–26), and later cities (Acts 22:25–29).

nation (biblical usage): a people or people group; i.e., the nations of the Canaanites, Hittites, Amorites, Perizzites, Hivites, and Jebusites (Jud. 3:1–5). Today we might speak of the German nation as opposed to the country of Germany. Individuals from the German nation also live in Poland, Russia, etc., and individuals from other nations live in Germany, such as Turks, Arabs, etc.

people group: A significantly large sociological grouping of individuals who perceive themselves to have a common affinity with one another. From the viewpoint of evangelization, this is the largest possible group in which the gospel can be spread without encountering barriers of understanding or acceptance.[2] Usually more than one people group is found in each country. In the country of Afghanistan, there are Pashtun, Tajik, Hazara, Uzbek, etc. And often a people group is found in more than one country. Uzbeks live in Uzbekistan, Afghanistan, Kazakhstan, Kyrgyzstan, Russia, etc. These realities, and biblical terminology, encourage us to strategize in terms of people groups rather than countries.

How Many Peoples Are in the World?

In this book, we will use the Joshua Project II list of peoples. This list identifies 17,081 people groups and considers what today are known as "ethno-cultural" groups, corresponding to a biblical nation or people.[3]

How Does God Bless a People?

Certainly we can only begin to imagine the full dimensions of all God has in mind when he says he will bless a people. But we do know some things with reasonable certainty.

It is Jesus who will bless the people. He began his public ministry by announcing, "The kingdom of heaven is near" (Matt. 4:17). The kingdom of heaven is simply the sphere in which God's rule is uncontested. Living in this sphere yields fullness of blessing to humans. Jesus is the door, the entryway into this kingdom (John 14:6).

His reign (affectionately carrying out his will and his ways) will increasingly permeate society. What he did and taught while he was on earth suggests something of what this might look like:

- The good news of the kingdom will be preached extensively.
- Growing numbers will respond and become his disciples.
- These disciples will mature to be like him from the inside out.
- They will welcome the rejected and abandoned.

- They will be channels of God's provision to the poor.
- The meek will be elevated to positions of influence.
- The sick will be healed.
- The power of evil spiritual forces will be broken.
- Godly business leaders will turn commercial enterprises into vehicles of kingdom extension.
- Godly government leaders will make government an instrument of righteousness.
- Opposition to Christ and his Church will increase.
- Times of persecution will be shortened.
- When Jesus returns, God's kingdom will fill the earth.

Jesus has called us to join him in this work. "Therefore go and make disciples of all nations" (Matt. 28:19). The last recorded words of Jesus are, "But you will receive power when the Holy Spirit comes on you; and you will be my witnesses in Jerusalem, and in all Judea and Samaria, and to the ends of the earth" (Acts 1:8).

Jesus will bless the people through his body, the Church. During Jesus' earthly life, he lived and ministered through his physical body. Since his resurrection, he has lived and ministered on earth through his new body. "Now you are the body of Christ, and each one of you is a part of it" (1 Cor. 12:27). Churches that effectively extend Christ's body and kingdom throughout a people share these four characteristics:

- They are personal (relational) in nature rather than institutional.
- They are spiritually vibrant.
- They are culturally relevant—received by and effective within their own culture.
- They are reproducing throughout their culture and among other cultures. They are outwardly rather than inwardly oriented.

Hanna and I were married in India. You could find churches in some parts of India whose buildings looked like they were shipped in from Europe. Once inside, you noticed Western-style pews, pulpits, and even boards for stating the attendance and offering. The entire scene looked out-of-place. After all, this was India.

The church where we were married was Indian, but not only in location. The building had a roof, but the sides were open with bamboo shades that could be drawn up and down. When you entered, you took your shoes off, just as you would when entering an Indian home. Men sat on one side and women on the other, reflecting the modesty of Indian ways. People sat on grass mats on the floor, like people generally do in India. In our wedding ceremony, there were no flowers. In Western culture, flowers are celebratory and beautiful. In the context of Hinduism, flowers speak of the worship of idols. We gladly submitted to the sensitivities of our Indian brothers and sisters in this. We wanted to do things their way. After all, this was India.

Meetings of the believers on Sunday morning did not revolve around the clock. That is a Western idea. But they would last for hours. The meetings were filled with worship, prayer, teaching, the Lord's Supper, and fellowship. They were powerful. And many were being attracted to faith in Christ through the vitality of his presence in their midst.

In India, churches with buildings and services rooted in Western practices were drying. Often there were only a handful of people in a large building. The churches (meetings of believers) that were part of the church movement in which we were married, were growing rapidly. They included many from a Hindu or Muslim background who had come to a life-changing personal knowledge of God through Jesus. Such churches were channels of God's blessings throughout the various cultures of India.

Local churches need to respond by planting churches among unreached peoples. Our most straightforward and comprehensive goal in blessing a people is to establish a grassroots movement of spiritually vibrant, culturally relevant churches spreading throughout the people.

Are There Peoples That Have Been Blessed?

Missiologists, those who study missions and missions strategies, have defined two broad categories of peoples:

reached people: A people that already has a viable indigenous community of believing Christians with adequate numbers and resources to evangelize their own people without outside, or cross-cultural, assistance. Mission initiatives from other regions can therefore safely be terminated.

> *An unreached people is a biblical nation among which our most straightforward and comprehensive goal in blessing a people has not yet been met. Therefore, to focus on starting churches among them is our most urgent priority.*

unreached people: A people that does not have a viable indigenous community of believing Christians with adequate numbers and resources to evangelize their own people without outside, or cross-cultural, assistance.[4]

A reached people, therefore, is a biblical nation among which our most straightforward and comprehensive goal in blessing a people has been met. This is *not* to say that there is no more work to do among them. There most certainly is! It is to say that the primary agent for doing this work is now in place. It is Christ himself, present in his churches, to an extent where the churches are able to minister to their own culture. As we develop new initiatives focused on completing Jesus' "all nations" commission, such peoples can be safely dropped from our list of targets.

Can We Identify Peoples Yet to Be Blessed?

An unreached people, on the contrary, is a biblical nation among whom our most straightforward and comprehensive goal in blessing a people has not yet been met. Therefore, to focus our energies on starting churches among them is our most urgent priority. The Joshua Project II list of peoples identifies 6,599 "least-reached" people groups.

---

[2]Patrick Johnstone and Jason Mandryk, *Operation World* (Waynesboro, Ga.: Gabriel, 2001), p. 757.
[3]Data available through Joshua Project II. Contact JoshuaProject.net or write P.O. Box 64080, Colorado Springs, Colo., 80962, for more information.
[4]Johnstone and Mandryk, *Operation World*, p. 759.

Now the body is not made up of one part but of many. (1 Cor. 12:14)

Establishing spiritually vibrant, culturally relevant, reproducing communities of Jesus' disciples, or churches, among every people on earth can seem a daunting task. Is this realistically doable? How? Our awesome Father, who is abounding in grace, intelligence, and ability, has not left us without a design. He has masterfully arranged for everything we need to be provided. Resources are there in glorious abundance.

Let's talk about the resource of manpower. Where do we find the people who can do this? This chapter is about the awesome potential of each individual

CHAPTER 4

Every Believer

In the last several decades, some good-hearted missions enthusiasts have promoted the idea that if a Christian really loves the Lord he or she will become a missionary. This reinforces two unhelpful, unbiblical ideas. The first is that God's people are found in two categories: religious professionals (pastors, missionaries, etc.) and everybody else. The second is that there is a pecking order of spirituality with missionaries on top.

In *Loving the Church...Blessing the Nations,* I have taken every opportunity to use the word *mission* rather than *missions.* Often when I am speaking in churches about completing world evangelization, I will ask the congregation to tell me what words come to their minds when they hear the word *missions* or *missionary.* The results are not encouraging.

People often begin with words they feel they are supposed to associate with missions. "Dedicated" is a common one. "Committed" is another. Some will say, "a life of faith." Some words are humorous, like "lions and tigers," "snakes," "pith helmets," or "slides of sunsets."

When I let the group keep going, I find people become more transparent. I begin to hear phrases like "no money," "old cars," "out-of-date neckties," and words like "suffering" or even "martyrdom." When words like "guilty" begin to surface, I know I have hit core honesty. The meanings triggered in many minds and emotions by *missions* and *missionary* are not appealing.

Mission on the other hand, correctly understood, carries powerful attraction. It speaks to us of purpose—God's purpose. God is a God with a mission, and participating with him in completing his mission is an invitation offered to every believer. *Mission* offers a God-sized challenge in which our lives can be meaningfully and joyously invested. It provides for our God-given need for significance. It can absorb all of our creativity. Missionary or non-missionary, it doesn't matter. Everyone has a place at the table.

Misunderstandings here keep most Christians from meaningful participation in God's purpose among all nations. We look inside ourselves, at the real person God made us to be, and we have no sense that we are to become a vocational missionary. If mission is the exclusive domain of missionaries, there is no meaningful way for us to become involved. Missions becomes a spectator sport in which most of us can only sit and watch the "religious professionals" perform. After a while, we lose interest.

I first met Ray when I was teaching a series on mission in his church. He came to several voluntary meetings, obviously interested. I suggested we have lunch together. As I started on my salad, I asked him to tell me his story.

Ray had made a number of genuine attempts at more traditional kinds of Christian service. "I used to be a deacon in a Baptist church," I remember him saying. "They asked us to do visitation, so I would go every week. They said people were just waiting to receive Christ." He paused, "Well, I never found anyone just waiting to receive Christ when I visited them. All they were waiting for was for me to leave." Ray had obviously not been gifted as an evangelist. But, wait, how *had* God gifted my brother?

I asked him about his work. "I am an engineer," he continued. "Growing up, I always wondered why people brought me things to fix rather than fixing them themselves. I slowly realized that fixing things is easier for me than for most people. I studied civil engineering at a university and went to work for a firm. My boss was taking under-the-table payments from city officials to get contracts. I told him that I was a Christian and could not do that. So I left. Since I was unemployed, I thought I would just go into practice on my own. That was a few years ago. I now own my own company with one hundred and twenty employees." He said it so matter-of-factly. The last thing he was trying to do was impress me. Here was a brother who loved Jesus, who had left a good-paying job to follow him, and who was sincerely trying to understand how he could serve. Boy, was Ray gifted! He was gifted to initiate, to lead, and to problem-solve. But, sadly, he was only finding expression for his gifting in the business world. I knew how desperately God's mission needed the kinds of gifts Ray had. But he was finding no outlet for them in the context of that mission. I grieved.

How profoundly tragic! Less than 0.1 percent of us have become foreign missionaries. If mission is the exclusive domain of vocational missionaries, where does that leave the other 99-plus percent of us?

God's gracious design is precisely the opposite. He includes *everyone*! He has created and endowed each person for true significance. Each of us is unique, with our own personal portfolio of natural abilities, spiritual gifts, and vocational expertise. God has fashioned every individual for a role in his kingdom that nobody else can fulfill and has placed us in an environment to count in ways no one else can.

We don't have to try to become somebody else, somebody we are not. Such attempts are incredibly counterproductive, even destructive. They show we are unable to trust that God really knew what he was doing and had our very best in mind when he made us the way we are. The person he designed each of us to be is just right.

> *To creatively express ourselves—the person we really are—in the context of God's worldwide purpose is the most fulfilling experience imaginable. It is the reason we are on earth!*

To creatively express ourselves—the person we really are—in the context of God's worldwide purpose is the most fulfilling experience imaginable. It is the reason we are on earth!

God doesn't buy in to clergy versus laity distinctions among Christians. This was never his idea! He designed one category of believers in Jesus: disciples. And it is disciples, with our breathtakingly gorgeous mosaic of God-given capacities, who form his manpower source for blessing the nations.

Having established that, it is important to clarify that vocational missionaries are absolutely included! One of them is writing these words. We are called to be disciples too. We are an essential part, a crucial part, of kingdom extension. But we are only a part, one part.

The question will be asked, "Don't we need more missionaries?" Absolutely. I would prefer, rather than to call forth individuals as missionaries, to call every believer (1) to embrace God's mission and (2) to fulfill the role God designed for him or her, indicated by his gracious calling and gifting. This of course includes all who are called to serve cross-culturally, but it goes way beyond that.

It is a way of gently affirming each person. It avoids the danger of setting one above the other. It steers us clear of language that can unintentionally be intrusive and manipulative. It will result in missionaries stepping forward, far more I think than otherwise, and will enrich the mission with the human resources it most certainly deserves and urgently needs.

> *I would prefer, rather than seeking to call forth individuals as missionaries, to call forth every believer (1) into God's mission and (2) into the role God designed for him or her.*

Starting new churches among unreached peoples is a comprehensive process, a process that beckons the contribution of every believer. If the only participants are missionaries, the mission will be severely deprived.

Maximizing the Mission Role of Every Believer

Every believer is called by God into ministry (Eph. 4:11–12). "Some," not "all," are given to be apostles, prophets, evangelists, pastors, and teachers. Their task is to prepare God's people (all of them!) for works of service. It is the fellowship of believers collectively that ministers. See the local church as the minister.

My twenty years of cross-cultural missionary service was divided into two main parts. First came five years in India, followed by fifteen years as the pioneer managing director of the two mission ships *Logos* and *Doulos*. These ships are part of the mission organization Operation Mobilization.

When God gave us the *Logos* toward the end of 1970, we had been asking him for a ship for world evangelization for some six years. But oh how little we fully realized what we had been asking! Operating a ship, with a full program of outreach and Christian discipleship, requires so much more than a group of enthusiastic, God-hungry Christian young people. It takes a captain, engineers, navigating officers, deck crew, electricians, carpenters, cooks, secretaries, managers, teachers, people skilled in communications, and lots and lots of willing and available hearts and hands.

During those years, the crew and staff with whom I had the privilege of serving enriched my life in unimaginable ways. They came from dozens of different countries and backgrounds. They taught me about God. They taught me that the Holy Spirit gifts each member of the body to serve God's purposes with fruitfulness and joy. They taught me about the church.

They taught me the principles of this chapter. I saw Jesus in them, up close and firsthand. In eternity I expect him to confer great honor on these unnamed, faithful servants.

Every believer is gifted by God for the ministry to which God has called him or her (1 Cor. 12:1). The idea that "every believer is called by God into ministry" can be frightening, especially for those who have had others try to get them to serve God through various forms of coercion and guilt.

> The idea that "every believer is called by God into ministry" can be frightening, especially for those who have had others try to get them to serve through coercion and guilt.

Our gracious Father has not called us to do anything he has not prepared and gifted us to do. And when we function in the gifts Christ has chosen for us, our experience is awesomely rich, fulfilling, and joyful. In fact, one of the ways we recognize how God is gifting us is by how fulfilled we feel when we are doing the things for which we have been gifted!

Ebbo joined the *Logos* team even before God gave us the ship. He is from Holland, where he worked as a welder in a Dutch shipyard. When we took possession of the vessel, he joined the deck crew. It was soon clear that God had not only given Ebbo work skills but also leadership qualities and practical wisdom.

One of the positions on *Logos* that we had difficulty filling was that of chief steward. The chief steward is responsible for all the food and accommodation functions on board. The job on *Logos* was different in some important ways from being chief steward on a regular ship. Yes, we needed management and discipline and excellence. But we also needed understanding and grace and a set of values and policies that honored and served Christian community.

We took a risk the day we signed Ebbo on ship's articles as chief steward. But he was God's choice, and God came through. He had gifted and prepared his servant well. Under Ebbo's leadership, the community on *Logos* enjoyed a season of refreshment, stability, and peace. Ebbo grew and developed in this role. He became part of the team who pioneered the second ship, *Doulos*, and then he moved with us to Germany to start the OM Ships headquarters where he oversaw the steward departments on both ships.

There is a diversity of gifts and ministries (1 Cor. 12:14). The well-intended idea that "everybody should be a missionary" violates this truth. God in his wisdom made generous provision in the Church for a rich diversity of natural abilities, spiritual gifts, and learned expertise. Trying to make everybody the same disregards Christ's headship of the Church. He is the author of diversity. He chooses what role each one is to play. Otherwise, we have our design, not his.

Recognizing and celebrating diversity affirms and liberates God's people. God's leaders are responsible to (1) recognize the ways in which individuals are being gifted, (2) affirm them in these gifts, (3) develop their capacity to

> *God is the author of diversity. He chooses what role each one is to play. Otherwise, we have our design, not his.*

effectively express their gifts, and (4) structure opportunities that allow these gifts to be deployed.

Beth is a wife, mother, and grandmother. She is from Indiana. I don't know how much time she ever spent outside the state before her church began to focus on church planting among an unreached people group in Central Asia. She and her husband Terry, a heating and air conditioning engineer, became involved in the church's process early on. They helped in the screening of applicants for the church's long-term church planting team. They took part in short-term teams the church sent to the target people group each summer to teach English as a second language.

Once the long-term church planting team was in place, Beth and Terry became part of a group of coaches for the team. The church wisely put in place a coaching visit every six months for encouragement and pastoral care. Hanna and I were asked to be part of this group of coaches. We traveled to Central Asia with Beth and Terry and watched them in action.

We saw God's hand on them. Leadership and cross-cultural gifting in Beth, in some aspects dormant and unseen in Indiana, emerged and flourished. The day came when Hanna and I told the church there was no longer a need for us to coach the team. We would coach the coaches. People like Beth knew far more than they thought they knew. God had gifted them for this work, and their gifts had been honed and developed through a church planting initiative born within their church. God, you are awesome!

Planting churches among unreached peoples is a complex process. It calls forth every gift. It woos the contribution of every believer. Apostolic-type church planting teams, which will be raised up and sent forth to unreached peoples, are merely the tip of the iceberg. Visualize an overall process of initiation, strategy development, implementation, management, pastoral support, and funding, and you will begin to see a wide range of roles, each of which is a channel for involvement.

Ted is a businessman in Beth's church. God hasn't called him to go to Central Asia. He has called him to be a businessman in Indiana. What role could a businessman in Indiana play in a church planting initiative in Central Asia?

As the church studied the needs of the people group to whom they had been called, comparing them with the individuals who were interested in the long-term team, they decided to design their initial approach around medical work. They formed a separate 501(c)(3) organization to facilitate and serve this approach. Later in this book, we discuss viewing this kind of organization as an apostolic structure.

Here Ted found his role. His business experience and role in the church ideally prepared him to serve as the chairman of the board of this organization. The organization has proven to be essential to the success of this initiative. Now, several years later, a small group of believers has been born in Central Asia, and the work is still growing. Other churches have joined the initiative. Ted's role in the facilitating organization, and the roles of other board members, has been as much a part of the birth of this new church as the role of those who went to Central Asia.

Most Christians will not leave home and go someplace else to minister. In most cases, if God's people are to meaningfully participate in God's global mission, they must be affirmed, developed, and released in their ministry gifting right where they live, in the context of the community of believers of which they are a part. We must view churches as centers of mission vision and implementation. Indeed, there is a sense in which each local community of faith is to mature into a mission fellowship. Only in this way can we even begin to realize the total mobilization of God's people into God's purposes.

Russ is an attorney. He is one of the managing partners of a law firm. He is also an elder in his church. He is a graduate of the Naval Academy and spent time as a naval officer before beginning to practice law. The world is a familiar place for him, and he has a keen interest in missions.

> *We must view churches as centers of mission vision and implementation. Indeed, there is a sense in which each local community of faith is to mature into a mission fellowship.*

His church has focused on church planting among an unreached people group in Indonesia. Throughout the process, Russ has played a key role of support and encouragement. He has worked with other leaders in the church to oversee this initiative, to solve problems, and to develop strategy. He has made several visits to the team in Indonesia for the purpose of encouragement and pastoral care.

Now the church is beginning to develop a second church-planting focus on an unreached people group in Central Asia. Hanna and I had the privilege of going on a prayer and survey trip to Central Asia with Russ and the other elders. The vital role Russ and these elders are playing in church planting initiatives in two countries and two unreached people groups is made possible only because these initiatives are rooted in the fellowship of their church.

Most Christians are called and gifted by God not for going but for sending or support. Examples of gifts and ministries needed in the process of support are

serving	showing mercy	healing
teaching	words of wisdom	helping
encouraging	faith	administration
giving	prophecy	pastoring
leading	intercession	

Many unevangelized cultures are effectively entered for a long-term basis through secular roles. Here are a few examples of viable roles in unreached societies:

student	teacher	health professional
engineer	consultant	business person
social scientist	lawyer	investor
retired person	researcher	travel agent

Where would we go to find believers proficient in such vocational roles?

Most believers will only find fulfillment in ministry when they are integrated into a group. A vast majority of Christians are frustrated in the area of ministry. They find no outlet to meaningfully express how they are gifted. The individualism that has deeply formed the perspective of Western cultures influences us to think almost entirely of ourselves. We think in terms of "my" gifts or "my" ministry. But most spiritual gifts and ministries cannot function

> *The individualism in Western cultures influences us to think almost entirely of ourselves. But most spiritual gifts and ministries cannot function alone. They are not designed that way.*

alone. They are not designed that way. Each gift, each ministry, and each person is to minister in relationship with other gifts, ministries, and people. Their potential will only be brought to full effectiveness when they are integrated into a ministering group, a mission community.

One Woman's Story

One evening after speaking to a group about the challenge of unreached peoples, several individuals had questions. I noticed one woman with a troubled expression, waiting off to the side until the others were through.

When we had a chance to talk, she expressed how deeply she desired to minister among unreached peoples. But she did not know how to go about it. I asked her to tell me how she sensed God had gifted her. She said she believed she had the gift of helping. I then felt led to ask her about her family situation. She said she was a single mother of two.

Then she said something that made me so very sad. She said, "I have been to Bible school, and I feel guilty that I am not using my Bible school training for the Lord."

How does a single mother of two, gifted by Jesus with the gift of helping, minister effectively among unreached peoples? One thing is for sure; she can't do it by herself. God's design for her, and for the rest of us, is to be integrated into a group that is ministering among unreached peoples. It is in the context of the ministering group that her gift of helping will be maximized. And for this woman, and for most of us, that ministering group will almost certainly be her home church.

Both sending and going are best done in groups. The New Testament describes for us two groups within the body of Christ: a local church is an example of a sending group, and a team is an example of a going group. We will look more closely at groups in the next three chapters.

Conclusion

During the reformation of the church in sixteenth century Europe, one of the passions of the reformers was to make the Word of God accessible to every believer. We now live in a time when God's leaders are increasingly recognizing that we must make the *work of God* accessible to every believer.

As the potential contribution of each believer is recognized, affirmed, developed, and released, a groundswell of joyful service will move across the earth, and Jesus will be proclaimed, known, worshipped, and loved among all nations.

> *During the reformation of the church, the reformers wanted to make the Word of God accessible to every believer. We now live in a time when God's leaders recognize that we must make the work of God accessible to every believer.*

After this I looked and there before me was a great multitude that no one could count, from every nation, tribe, people and language, standing before the throne and in front of the Lamb.... And they cried out in a loud voice: "Salvation belongs to our God, who sits on the throne, and to the Lamb" (Rev. 7:9–10).

In God's design, the manpower for global mission comes not from one small group of Christian disciples (vocational missionaries) but from every believer. In this chapter we have considered the individual. We now turn our attention to the interplay between the individual and the group.

All the believers were together and had everything in common. (Acts 2:44)

To God, each individual has awesome significance. He calls and gifts us individually. He woos us toward vital participation with him in his global purpose. But there is a sickness that is associated with focusing on the individual that does not come from God—individualism.

In modern, Western cultures individualism pervades and molds our thought patterns. What will I as an individual choose to do in terms of my schooling, my career, my residence, my money, my discretionary time, and my retirement? We view these choices as the rightful domain of the individual.

We bring this perspective into our understanding of how to live the Christian life. We view following Christ as an individual matter. I choose a church to attend based on which one best meets my needs and reflects my preferences. I focus on how I personally can grow, what speakers I like, and what books minister to me. In deciding how I will minister, I follow personal inclinations.

What is the biblical balance to individualism?

CHAPTER 5
Christian Community

In the last chapter, we concentrated on the individual. We discovered awesome truths about God's delight in, call upon, and gifting of each person. But we also found that the individual alone is incomplete. Focusing on the individual introduces us inextricably to the indispensable role of the group.

God Places Us in Groups

When individualism dominates our thought patterns, it leaves us largely unaware of the reality of the group. And this impacts our well being in some very negative ways. For example, God has placed each of us in a family. How we relate with other members of this family will impact us deeply. When we are unaware of this, or treat it lightly, we open ourselves up to real damage.

God has also placed each individual believer in his family—the body of Christ. There are crucial dimensions of our life with Jesus that can only be lived out in the context of this group. If we do not realize this, and take the necessary initiatives in light of it, we will never fully mature as Christians. No, that is not overstated. Yes, what we are talking about here is that crucial.

If we never fully mature as Christians, we will not be effective in expressing our role in God's plan as he expands his kingdom. Healthy understanding of and participation in Christian community is crucial to effective mission.

In the New Testament, as indicated in the last chapter, we are presented with two foundational groups within the body of Christ: local churches and ministry teams. We will consider each of these more deeply in the following two chapters, but first, let's examine some characteristics that make Christian communities so powerful, especially in extending God's kingdom among all nations.

For the moment, we will investigate Christian community as a condition, a state shared by a group of individual believers.

Why Is Christian Community So Powerful?

Christian community creates a context for powerful corporate worship. And worship is at the very heart of mission. In fact, God's mission can be articulated in terms of worship: "All nations will come and worship before you" (Rev. 15:4).

Worship is a crucial occupation for us as we go about the work of global kingdom proclamation. Christ's commission is yet to be completed because of the existence of opposing spiritual forces. God has an enemy, and although this enemy is a defeated foe, he is committed to causing as much evil and destruction as he can before his end comes. Against this enemy we battle. We fight in the realm of the spirit, and worship is a key component in this fight. During an aggressive evangelistic and church planting campaign, battling powers of evil arrayed against them, Paul and Silas engaged in prayer and worship—activities designed to counter the spiritual opposition they were facing (Acts 16:25).

Groups allow for spiritual dimensions in worship that are unavailable to individuals. God inhabits the praises of his people. Worship creates space for God. It drives back the presence and power of evil. It is a vital activity in the proclamation of the kingdom throughout the earth. Every believer

> *For many, worship might be the most important role they play in the purposes of God.*

is invited to this banquet. For many, it might be the most important role they play in the purposes of God (Acts 4:23–31).

The point here is certainly not to minimize the value of individual worship. Absolutely not! It is to underline the special nature and power available in united group worship and to strategize for its use in activities of kingdom extension.

Christian community creates a context for vitality and sustainability in prayer. The disciples asked Jesus to teach them to pray. He did so not just by giving talks about prayer but also by demonstrating the practice of prayer. He did this almost exclusively in group settings. He allowed them to observe his own prayer life. In the garden of Gethsemane, the hour of his greatest need, he took a group with him into prayer.

We learn much about prayer from one another, especially from those more experienced than we are. As we pray together, we experience God's answers together. This deepens our bonding with God and with one another. We share a common experience of God. Our faith is strengthened. Our knowledge of him and his ways deepens.

Group prayer also provides for sustainability. For most people, extended times of prayer are much more doable in the context of a group than alone. We find encouragement from one another. Prayer, like worship, is central to how we combat the forces of evil against God and the advance of his kingdom. It is crucial to learn how to enter effectively into this sanctuary of the spirit and to remain for extended times.

Christian community creates a context for complementing each other's gifts. The truth that God has gifted me has a corollary: there are crucial areas where I have not been gifted. In these areas I am vulnerable and needy. Christ has gifted me not for my own benefit but for the benefit of others. Spiritual gifts work by love. That is why 1 Corinthians 13, one of the most exalted biblical statements on love, is placed in the midst of an extended discussion of spiritual gifts. I have been gifted for the purpose of practically loving others and using my gifts to meet their needs.

Then how are my needs to be met? They are met through the gifts of others. I am dependent on my brothers and sisters to meet my needs, and they depend on me to help meet their needs. This is how Jesus designed his church. But if I have not been grafted into a group of Christians, my needs will not be met fully, and I will be frustrated in ministry. I will find no meaningful way to express the gifts Christ has given me.

I spent the first twenty years of my missionary career with all my focus on the task. I didn't believe in days off or vacations! People were lost and time was short. And God, in his astounding grace, brought about some beautiful fruit through my ministry. Just because God is using us doesn't mean everything is right!

When I was forty-five years old, I hit the wall. I was emotionally and spiritually exhausted, disoriented, angry, and hurt. I entered a season where I was of little use to anyone. Nothing was working anymore, and I did not know why that was so or what I should do.

God brought me into close relationship with a church rich in pastoral gifts. There were brothers and sisters there who loved me, and through areas of gifting (and maturity) that I did not have, they ministered to me in profound ways. God used them in healing, correction, encouragement, and blessing. Any fruit that the Holy Spirit is bearing through my gifts now carries in it a contribution from these pastorally gifted brothers and sisters. The fact that they lacked in areas of my strengths only makes this truth all the more beautiful.

Christian community creates a context for nurture and support. Mission tends to attract people who are oriented toward a task, who want to get the job done, and who are not primarily concerned with, or even aware of, their own needs. There is part of this that is wonderful. Jesus was not primarily oriented toward meeting his own needs either. He came to lay down his life for others.

But God, in his great wisdom and mercy, knows how easily we can get out of balance. He created us human, with human needs and limitations. He expects these to be respected. He has placed among us brothers and sisters whose calling and gifting is to care.

People with a strong pastoral gifting may not be the first to respond to a radical challenge to mission, to a call to be missionaries. But watch them come forward when they see God's servants wounded and needy! There are casualties in this battle, and God has placed among us those gifted by the Holy Spirit to minister healing to the wounded. Jesus has graciously distributed among us gifts of healing, caring, discernment, and mercy to keep us going in health for the long haul. The diversity in the church is designed to bring a godly balance between radically forsaking all and the appropriate care of individuals.

Christian community creates a context for maturing character. All of the different traits the New Testament tells us are components of Christ's character, and hence the character of the maturing disciple, come together in love. Mature in love, and everything else will fall into place. Jesus told us that the Law and the Prophets are fulfilled by loving God with all our hearts and loving our neighbor as ourselves (Matt. 22:35–40). The epistles teach that virtues such as compassion, kindness, humility, gentleness, patience, bearing with each other, and forgiving one another are all bound together in love (Col. 3:12–14).

Love is a relational activity. It can only be learned and expressed as we relate to other people, to God, and to other human beings. We can neither love nor learn to love by ourselves. By the time a Christian comes to understand that love is supreme, he has been formed by the habits of thought, emotion, and action that sabotage love. The Christian must become aware of these patterns and replace them with patterns of relating to others that reflect the person of Christ. This takes place in the context of a community. We cannot fully mature when we are isolated.

Christian community creates a context for hearing God. God speaks in a number of ways—through the Scriptures, through nature, through the Holy Spirit, etc. He also speaks through our

> *The Christian must be aware of the patterns that sabotage love and replace them with patterns that reflect Christ. This takes place in the context of a community. We cannot fully mature when we are isolated.*

other brothers and sisters. When we are alone, there is a greater danger of not hearing him correctly. Many cults have been formed by people who were convinced they had gained a new understanding of the Scriptures but were in fact in error. Others have been convinced that they heard the Holy Spirit but arrived at inaccurate interpretations of what they heard.

What protection do we have from being deceived? The group! When we believe we hear God speak, we are to look for confirmation from other godly men and women who walk with him and hear him too. In no less an issue than the timing of the release of God's chosen apostle to the Gentiles, God spoke through a group of prophets and teachers who were waiting upon him in worship (Acts 13:2). Some ten years earlier, in Acts 9:15–16, God had made it clear that Paul's calling was "to carry my name before the Gentiles and their kings and before the people of Israel." What was not yet clear was God's timing for this to begin. The answer came not to the individual Paul but to the group of leaders gathered in community.

Christian community creates a context where seekers can meet Jesus in his community. A beautiful scriptural picture of the power of the groups is found in Acts 2:42–47. This is what the life of Jesus looks like when it is spontaneously expressed. These folks had been to no conferences, read no books, and had no churches that they were using as models. The Holy Spirit simply fell and filled those who believed. They did what came naturally.

There was humility—a hunger to learn more about this new truth that had transformed them. There was personal caring. There was worship and the breaking of bread. There was communion with God and unhurried delight in prayer. There was the sharing of material possessions. Desire to be together was strong enough to cause them to congregate daily. Their shared life extended into their homes. The neighbors noticed all this and found it very attractive. Who wouldn't want to be part of something like this?

Luke adds, "And the Lord added to their number daily those who were being saved." What a gentle, natural, gracious description! Adding new believers to the group was something the Lord was doing. It sounds almost spontaneous. We read of no great evangelists here, no human striving or massive effort. Those without encountered Christ living in the midst of the group, and they were powerfully and redemptively drawn in. Many times the most powerful agent of evangelism is simply the life of Jesus lived out in the group.

Christian community creates a context for motivation to be sustained. It was not long before the infant Church encountered opposition. Peter and John were put in jail overnight then brought before the authorities and commanded not to speak any more in Jesus' name.

It is a serious thing to be committed to the proclamation of Christ's gospel among all peoples. God's enemy is not happy with such commitments and opposes those who make them. Many have begun in mission full of enthusiasm and hope only to be quickly brought up short. It is one thing to commit oneself to completing Christ's "all nations" mandate. It is quite another to sustain that commitment over time in personal victory and ministry fruitfulness.

Peter and John, having refused to bend before their opponents, returned to the fellowship of the church (Acts 4:23–31). There they found others who shared their purpose, fellowship in worship and prayer, and a common experience of the encouragement and empowerment of the Holy Spirit. This is not to suggest that the Lord does not meet the needs of the individual. He most certainly does! It is to highlight the resources provided by the group and to show how vital it is for us to see God's design. Powerful mission flows forth from community.

Christian Community Holds the Key to the Mobilization of the Church

In recent decades, there has been a growing recognition that in our strategies for completing world evangelization it is key for us to mobilize others. In keeping with our individualistic orientation, we have thought predominately in terms of mobilizing individuals.

I was part of a mission organization that followed this approach, and large portions of my time and energy for twenty years were spent mobilizing individuals. There is much in this that is very good and appropriate and that God uses wonderfully for his glory.

Recognizing the power of groups will suggest a paradigm shift to the missions mobilization movement. What if rather than focusing on individuals, we were to mobilize entire churches? This would pave the way for exponentially greater results than those possible by merely mobilizing individuals.

> *Recognizing the power of groups will suggest a paradigm shift to the missions mobilization movement. What if rather than focusing on individuals, we were to seek to mobilize entire churches?*

To him be glory in the church. (Eph. 3:21)

This book will strike many as primarily a statement about mission. There are actually two pillars to its foundation. The first is a call for the proclamation of the kingdom of God among all nations. The second is an appeal for a high view of the local church. Remove either one of those and you dismember the core message.

It is not as though these two are unrelated. As we enter the third millennium of the Christian era, there is widespread awareness that the energy and capacity of the mission movement would be appreciably enhanced if we could bring more local churches into meaningful participation.

To say that the church is an awesome resource is still an understatement, possibly somewhat condescending. She is more than that. She is a God-designed central player, a full partner. The vast majority of all the resources God has entrusted to his people—spiritual gifts, vocational expertise, life experience, capacity for spiritual warfare, financial reserves, etc.—he has placed in local churches.

To understand how to meaningfully incorporate local churches into global missions, we have to understand something more fundamental and important. We have to understand the church.

CHAPTER 6
The Local Church

Studying the characteristics of churches as they exist in one geographical area or social grouping can yield valuable information. But we must be careful with this approach. It can also lead us down some errant paths. The real issue is not, What are churches like in this particular area or among this defined group? More important is the question, What are the characteristics of the church as God designed her?

Characteristics of the Church

God designed the church to be Christ's earthly body. The miracle of the Incarnation is that God came to earth as a human being. For thirty-three years Jesus lived on earth bodily. He still does. He lives in the church. Do you want to see Christ? Look at the church. The church is a person. The church is Jesus.

"Saul was breathing out murderous threats against the Lord's disciples...He fell to the ground and heard a voice say to him, 'Saul, Saul, why do you persecute me?'" (Acts 9:1,4).

God designed the church to be a bride. The church is a person who is not yet fully mature. She is a beautiful, teen-age woman. There are, at this stage in her development, flaws, imperfections, and immaturities. She is being prepared for marriage to God's Son. Before Jesus returns to earth, the gospel must be preached to all nations, and the bride must be fully prepared (matured) for the wedding (Rev. 19:9). In a missions context, when we ask, "How can we mobilize the church?" it will be critically important for us to understand that the church is a bride—a woman. We must approach her differently than we would a man.

To mobilize a man, we might be rough and pushy. With a woman it is better to be gentle. With a man we might challenge. With a woman it is more appropriate and effective to woo. With a man we might demand a quick response. We will honor a woman by being patient. With a man we might give orders. With a woman we will need to, with integrity and tenderness, cultivate response.

We mobilize the church for mission by honoring her and affirming her beauty, wooing her gently, and giving her time to process our advances and arrive at her own conclusions. This will set the stage for her to be able to give herself fully to Christ. She is his bride, not ours. She is to give herself to him, not to our self-designed program. When the Church makes her own decision to give herself to Christ, the bridegroom, we have pure motivation for mission.

God designed churches to be families. He is receiving and adopting new members into his family from among all nations. Here individuals find forgiveness and acceptance by God and one another. The church is an agent of inner healing and transformation as her members live out, in humility and obedience, the teachings of Jesus who lives among them. The church is the earthly receptacle for God's purity, a light on a hill that cannot be hidden and that shines brilliantly into the darkness in which humanity is engulfed. *The church is a community of being.*

God designed churches to be agents of mission. They are made up of many members whom Jesus has graced with a rich diversity of gifts. As churches are nurtured toward maturity, Jesus fills them with the capacity to minister and endows them with spiritual authority and power. The gates of hell cannot prevail against them. Churches can grow into centers of ministry, with kingdom vision filling their members' hearts as Christ's life is shared among them. Churches can start new churches in their own localities and become staging points for kingdom initiatives focused on yet-to-be-blessed nations. *The church is a community of doing.*

God designed churches to be unique in culture and style. Each one is to authentically express Christ's call through the natural abilities, spiritual gifts, and life experiences of its members. The church's leaders violate it when they try to impose generalities from without, even if these come from other wonderful churches! The church is a unique, living organism, belonging only to Christ. His life is released in it by the free, creative expression of who it is in the sum of its members. It is as damaging to compare churches with one another as it is to compare individuals with each other. Inevitably, one appears better. This wounds the body. It is untrue. One is not better than the other, just different.

God's design for each church is to authentically express the culture in which it is rooted. This is far more foundational than a strategy for church growth. It is the church's essence. Jesus came to earth as God incarnate. He is still incarnate in the social context in which he is found. Christ ministers throughout a culture from the position of belonging in that culture.

God designed churches to share one essence. Each church authentically expresses God's design for all churches. Churches are beautiful, the fullest manifestation of Jesus on earth until he returns. Churches are gifted, richly equipped with a diversity of spiritual gifts. Churches are families endowed with resources to nurture and heal. Churches are agents of mission designed to herald the message of God's dear Son in their own locality and among all peoples.

Present Imperfections

Many will hear these words as far too idealistic and out of touch with reality. To be sure, the churches with whom we are all familiar embody various levels of imperfection. When a believer chooses to sin, he not only brings damage to himself but also harms the body. The church's leaders can mislead, and its teachers can teach falsely. This causes further damage. Fellowship can be rendered lifeless when we try to make the church a corporation or an institution—structural forms antithetical to God's pattern.

None of this alters the magnificence of God's original design. On the contrary, it provides a backdrop that highlights the breathtaking dimensions of God's grace in the face of human waywardness. God will perfect his Church. The bride will be ready when the time for her wedding has come. God is calling forth an army of leaders

> God is calling forth an army of leaders who will love, nurture, teach, and lead local churches into the exalted role he has ordained for them.

who will love, nurture, teach, and lead local churches into the exalted role he has ordained for them.

Churches Reproducing New Churches

It is reasonable to conceptualize churches as centers that initiate church planting among unreached peoples. Why?

Each member of the church can participate in the mission. Most believers are not going to quit their jobs, complete theological education, raise financial support, sell their homes, take their children out of schools, and move somewhere else in order to take part in God's purposes. It is not their Father's will for them to do so. If their contribution is to be made, it will be right where they live in the context of their church.

Each spiritual gift, natural talent, and vocational skill in the church are available to the mission. When mission implementation is anchored in churches, the rich diversity of spiritual gifts, natural skills, and life expertise among all God's people becomes available to the task.

Christians who work in secular careers are naturally linked with opportunities among the target people group. Many unreached societies can only be effectively engaged through secular employment. When a fellowship of believers together owns a common mission, individuals within the fellowship will begin to think about how they might use their vocations to advance the common purpose. Ownership is a powerful motivator. *Those who work cross-culturally are connected with people gifted in pastoral care.* Healthy churches are blessed with effective shepherds. This is God's provision for his people. The process of leaving one's home culture and being transplanted into another is quite stressful, for an individual or for a family. People focused on the task can be unaware of inner needs in themselves, much less in their families and co-workers. Not understanding how to minister to personal issues has caused many committed cross-cultural witnesses to suffer unnecessary pain and failure. God has made provisions within churches for the nurture of his servants.

Mission is carried out in a context that provides resources for character development. Over time, godly character is the single most important issue in the effectiveness of those sent to start churches among unreached peoples. It is the most important area of training for cross-cultural service. It is far too crucial to be minimized. Without it, we will fail. Character grows over time in the context of committed, transparent relationships. In this environment, what is inside us comes to the surface, and we can receive ministry in grace and truth.

The church develops a grassroots ownership of the mission. This paves the way for a groundswell of investment. Over time, most believers find it hard to identify with what someone else is doing thousands of miles away, regardless of how significant and well intended it is. We can own the things we are doing much more easily than we can own what someone else is doing. And with ownership comes investment. The key to mobilization is ownership. Who owns the mission? Those who feel ownership of

> *The key to mobilization is ownership. Those who feel ownership of it will be motivated to invest themselves in it.*

it will be motivated to invest themselves in it.

Mission teams are mentored in the principles of church life. This is powerful preparation for starting strong, healthy churches. If new churches are to be the end product, to start them, let's send people who have proven themselves in the whole range of church life. The dynamics of a local church are different in some important aspects from those of a parachurch organization. Healthy churches are ideal environments for emerging leaders to be mentored and trained by older, proven leaders.

Those gifted to innovate and problem solve are able to participate. The complexities of reaching the still unreached require new strategies. I was recently in a fairly new church filled with university professors, health professionals, and design engineers with the Ford Motor Company. In urging them to consider choosing an unreached people group for church planting, I said to them, "If you can figure out how to design, produce, and market a top-performing car, you can figure out how to plant churches among one unreached people group!" Innovative skills developed and matured

> *When missionaries hit the wall in their personal lives, to whom do they turn? Ideally they return to a sending community—a local church.*

in the marketplace have an awesome potential when applied to the challenge of expanding God's kingdom among unreached peoples. Such skills are one of the resources of the local church.

There is a base for developing a common ministry philosophy and establishing personal bonding. Weakness in the areas of ministry philosophy and personal bonding has wrecked many teams. An effective team is made up of many people who happen to be in the same location, which is made possible if a team comes from the same church. The members share relational bonds and a common sense of purpose. These take time and personal investment with one another to establish, but once they are present, they take teams through the rough spots that cause individuals on their own to stumble.

The sending constituency is more effectively involved. Contrast two hundred names on a prayer letter list with two hundred friends who share their lives and are bonded with a team in vision and relationship. I once met with a wonderful missionary family who had ministered among an unreached people for fifteen years. Although their commitment to the Lord and the lost was beyond question, they were in deep personal trauma. When I asked them to tell me about their home church, they looked at me with blank expressions. They had no home church! Their sending constituency was a list of names and addresses on a mailing list rather than a community of people who loved them, felt committed to them, and were positioned to respond to their needs.

He appointed twelve . . . that they might be with him and that he might send them out to preach.
(Mark 3:14)

We see two foundational groups in the New Testament. One is the local church. The local church's primary function is one of nurture, although it also has a missional component. The end result of nurture without mission (purpose or task are both synonymous) is ingrownness. It is not nurture at all because its fruits are selfishness and entrenched immaturity.

The second New Testament group is the team. The team's primarily function is one of mission (or purpose or task), although it has a nurture component. The end result of mission without nurture is burnout. It is not mission at all because its fruits are failure and the wounding of people.

How can we better understand these biblical structures?

CHAPTER 7
Serving in Teams

In developing strategies to reproduce churches among unreached peoples, it is crucial that teams are central in any approach. The unmistakable pattern of the book of Acts is that apostolic teams went forth to proclaim the kingdom and to plant new churches. In the area of support, teams are also vital.

What Is a Team?

Perhaps we should begin with a working definition. A team is a relatively small group of people who share a common purpose, a relational bonding, and effective leadership. The wording is intentionally flexible.

A team is something living and organic, rather than rigid and predictable. We could think, in the first instance, of two to thirteen people. Jesus said that where two or three are gathered together, he is in their midst. Certainly a married couple is meant to be a team. And on the high end, Jesus called together a team of thirteen, composed of Jesus as leader and twelve disciples.

Are these numbers rigid? No. Can there be teams of fourteen? Sure. At one point I led a team of three hundred from thirty different countries. But the larger teams become, the more they tend to break down into subteams. Even among the twelve, there seemed to be a subgroup of Peter, James, and John. A team of twenty will almost certainly be composed in reality of two to three subteams.

Teams have purpose. They do things. They produce results. They are task-oriented. Purpose brings teams together and serves as a powerful incentive for them to stay together. The apostle Paul and his teams shared a compelling purpose: to make Christ known among the nations.

Teams have relational bonding. Purpose alone will not build strong teams. People also need relationship. A soulless focus on task without

> *It is impossible to be committed to God's purpose without being committed to people. God's purpose is people.*

being responsive and committed to others will not endure. This is especially true among believers who share a kingdom purpose. It is impossible to be committed to God's purpose without being committed to people. God's purpose *is* people.

Teams have effective leadership. A great strength of teams is the ability to apply diverse spiritual gifts and practical skills to a common task. One might ask if there is a list of spiritual gifts that should be represented on an ideal church-planting team among an unreached people. Our experience is that God always surprises us in the array of gifts he brings together. We are unable to formulate any universal pattern except to say that teams form around leaders and are motivated and kept together by them. Godly leadership is not bossy or controlling but caring and serving. Team members are often more capable and gifted in their areas of strength than the leader. The leader's area of strength is the capacity to keep high-energy people working together in health and unity toward a shared purpose.

Why Is Team Ministry Preferable?

The team format is the model we find in the New Testament. Jesus formed his disciples into a team. He sent them out in teams. Paul carried out his apostolic church-planting ministry among unreached peoples through teams. These are powerful, inescapable models. What do they say to us today?

Teams allow a diversity of gifts to be applied to a common purpose. Think of what we expect of today's missionary who serves among an unreached people. He or she is expected to be

- theologically trained.
- an effective communicator to the culture of his or her supporters.
- fluent in at least one foreign language.
- effective in living in and communicating with another culture.
- able to meet family and personal needs in high stress situations.
- competent to work in another vocational field.

Is all this best achieved by one individual working alone or by a team of people sharing responsibilities and encouraging each other?

Teams carry an enhanced capacity to engage in spiritual warfare. The daily work of kingdom proclamation triggers daily counter responses from the enemy. He intends to stop the ministry and bring harm to the messengers. Through corporate worship and intercession, we enter into God's protected place and address the opposition we are facing. Those doing this work as individuals alone are unnecessarily exposed to increased danger.

Teams can provide nurture and pastoral care for its members. Team members are able to give each other a crucial ingredient for long-term effectiveness—the love and affirmation of God expressed through his people. Individuals working alone cannot give this to themselves. How does this correlate to the high rate of missionary dropout that so concerns observers? Increasingly, cross-cultural teams are discovering the benefit of having a team member or couple whose primary role is pastoral care.

Team life fosters character growth. Even in local churches, especially larger ones, it is possible to hide. This is much more difficult on a team. Unhealthy habits of behaving and relating will surface. When they do, a context of caring

> *Team members are able to give each other a crucial ingredient for long-term effectiveness—the love and affirmation of God expressed through his people.*

commitment and pastoral competence can open the way for personal growth. Many have looked back on their experience on a team as being one that was difficult but also very fruitful for their own maturity. Team life can be an awesome preparation for marriage.

Healthy teams are small communities, and Christian community is one of the most powerful agents for evangelism. A team is often the first chance a person has to encounter Christ as he lives among his people. Two of the most fruitful church planting movements in history were in essence the kingdom of God spreading through small Christian communities. Following the New Testament era, the gospel permeated the Roman Empire in the midst of severe persecution. This phenomenon was not generally catalyzed or led by well-known or especially endowed Christian evangelists and leaders. The kingdom spread as a grassroots movement of small, believing communities. It was said of Christians, "See how they love one another." In modern times we have seen this same phenomenon in China.

The ship *Doulos* first visited Buenos Aires, Argentina, in June 1979. She carried a mobile Christian community—a team of over three hundred believers from more than thirty countries. My wife Hanna and I were among them. Hanna had five first cousins living in Buenos Aires. They were all Jewish. They came on board, with their spouses, children, and, in some cases, grandchildren. What a family reunion!

One day, several of them were visiting with us in our cabin. All of a sudden one said, "There is a peace on this ship. Where does that peace come from?"

Peace? It felt like excessive activity, noise, people, and stress to us. But what was our daily reality, so normal that we hardly noticed it, was very unusual and attractive to these sensitive non-Christians. They were meeting Jesus for the first time as he lived in the midst of his community.

Then Barnabas went to Tarsus to look for Saul, and ... he brought him to Antioch. (Acts 11:25–26)

Through the centuries, initiatives to complete Christ's "all nations" mandate have yielded mixed results. On the one hand, we must celebrate the progress made these two thousand years. On the other hand, it has been two thousand years! Thousands of nations still don't have the good news of the kingdom readily accessible to them. Entire areas of the earth, such as the 10/40 Window, are home to people groups designated as unreached. Why is this?

To offer quick, simplistic solutions would be insensitive, naïve, and unhelpful. Questions continue to burn in our minds and hearts: Why has progress been so slow? Is it only a matter of the spiritual opposition? Are we just to keep going and try harder? Or are there critical factors that we have not yet understood?

In addition to an "all nations" mandate, has God given us an "all nations" design as to how it is to be implemented?

When it comes to God's purposes among the nations, one figure stands head and shoulders above all others. Saul of Tarsus, later renamed Paul, was God's specially chosen apostle for blazing the trail in this great endeavor. When we look carefully at God's ways with Paul, do we see components of his design for blessing the nations?

CHAPTER 8

The Church at Antioch

Obviously we must be careful here. God is a God of broad principle and gracious framework. Legalistic formulas cannot contain him. His ways allow for differences in people, circumstances, and history. He leaves many decisions to us, and then honors them himself. In many areas, he may be more flexible than we are! But God's ways do stand in clear contrast to the ways of man. His ways yield fruitfulness and blessing. Ignoring them brings damage and dysfunction.

The context of Paul's release into the mature phase of his ministry life is described in Acts 13:1–3. This is an important passage of Scripture, a seam in the fabric of New Testament history. Up to this point, although God's heart for the Gentiles has been clearly and repeatedly articulated, the focus of action has been on Israel. This focus is now about to shift.

I want to carefully suggest some design components in God's approach to blessing the nations. This treatment will certainly not be exhaustive, and I do not mean to suggest that God is always obligated to work this way. I do not believe he is. God is God—free and creative, responding personally and always valuing issues of the heart above external methodology. But my experience tells me that there is scriptural direction and spiritual power when we design mission initiatives around these components.

Components in God's Design

When we look more closely at the words of Acts 13:1–3, what do we actually discover in the text?

We discover a church. "In the church at Antioch" (Acts 13:1). God took the leader he personally chose to bear his name before the Gentiles and located him in the midst of a local fellowship of believers (Acts 9:15).

Paul was brought to Antioch in a ministry role, but this must have been a season of further preparation for him as well. He would have been familiar with the life and practices of the Jewish synagogue, but we have little record of him gaining such experience of the body of Christ. The work to which God was calling Paul involved planting new churches among unreached peoples. This required experience and training in church life and ministry. The church at Antioch provided this for him.

> *The work to which God was calling Paul involved planting new churches among unreached peoples. This required experience and training in church life and ministry.*

It was in a church that Paul

- spent his final season of preparation.
- had God's call confirmed by other spiritually mature leaders.
- heard God's timing for his release.
- saw his first apostolic team come together.
- received spiritual covering in prayer.
- launched his first initiative among the Gentiles.
- found refuge to refuel for future initiatives (Acts 14:26–28).

And it was new churches that were the mature fruit of his

activities.

We discover prophets and teachers. "There were prophets and teachers" (Acts 13:1). We could call them leaders in a church, but the words Luke chooses here, guided by the Holy Spirit, are more precise: prophets and teachers. He subsequently identifies two of them, Barnabas and Paul, as apostles (Acts 14:14). How are we to understand these terms?

I write keenly sensitive that significant portions of the Church hold the view that the ministry of the apostle and prophet ended with the New Testament era. I hold the churches and their leaders who take this view in high regard. I want to exercise every caution in what I write not to cause further division in Christ's body. I write as a learner desiring to understand more and sure that I have much more to learn. I do not write to offer rigid, final, controversial answers. I am very aware that Scripture warns that those of us who teach must be responsible for the consequences of what we teach (James 3:1). I invite the reader to journey with me as a partner, friend, and co-learner.

I have spent over thirty-five years in missions, searching for keys to the completion of world evangelization. Along the way, I have become more and more convinced that one critical key is leadership; more precisely, a certain kind of leadership.

Leaders called by God, gifted by him to initiate kingdom breakthroughs and empowered by the Holy Spirit, make kingdom expansion happen. When these leaders are not present, godly people who sincerely desire the right things can become frustrated and defeated. Nothing is happening! Why? Is it because those who carry God's call and gifts to make it happen are not part of the equation? Is a crucial part of God's design not being followed?

For God's kingdom to penetrate new spaces

> *Leaders called by God, gifted by him to initiate kingdom breakthroughs, and empowered by the Holy Spirit make kingdom expansion happen.*

in the human mosaic, it will require more than man's will power, plans, programs, and formulas. My life's work has become responding to churches when they ask, "How can our church initiate church planting among an unreached people?" I cannot give them a complete answer without saying, "A crucial component is to have the right leader. If you don't have God's leader, it is not yet God's time for you to do this."

The leaders we refer to have an unshakable sense of God's call upon them. They are visionaries, but the vision they carry is God given and not from man. They are big-picture thinkers. They carry God's message and are gifted by him to initiate new works, to lay foundations for these works, and to identify, develop, and release new leaders for these works. None of this contradicts what was said earlier about teams. Every leader needs a team. Every team needs a leader.

What shall we call these leaders? Many terms are available from the secular world. But if these leaders are essential to God's global purpose, surely they are found in the New Testament! What term(s) does the New Testament use to identify them? What characteristics describe them? I don't believe God is hung up on terminology, but if the New Testament has a word for something are we not on safer ground to use it?

My life journey in God's work has placed me among mission organizations and local churches on five continents in some one hundred countries. It has brought me to a place where I cannot avoid the conviction that the ministry roles of Ephesians 4:11–13—apostles, prophets, evangelists, pastors, and teachers—are operating among us today. God's grace must pour through these chosen and God-gifted ministers if God's kingdom is to flow into new societies. To be sure, there have been abuses and misapplications of these incredibly precious callings. We must address and correct those abuses. Foundations here are in need of repair.

> *Every leader needs a team.*
> *Every team needs a leader.*

A note of clarification may be in order at this point. Jesus Christ is the foundation of the church. There can be no other (1 Cor. 3:11). He included the original twelve apostles and the prophets in laying that foundation (Eph. 2:20). This included the completion of the New Testament cannon. The original foundation of the church has been laid, and New Testament revelation is complete.

That said, every new work of God—every church, charity, school, hospital, mission organization, etc.—requires the laying of foundations. These foundations must be laid upon and judged by the original foundation laid by Christ, the apostles, and prophets.

It is beyond the scope of this book to consider each of the Ephesians 4 ministry roles in depth. It is my understanding that leaders called to initiate present-day works of God are the same kind of leaders who fulfilled an apostolic role in the New Testament. There are those, in addition to the twelve, whom the Scripture designates apostles. Because of its crucial role, we will pursue an understanding of apostolic ministry more thoroughly in the next chapter.

We discover worship. "They were worshipping the Lord" (Acts 13:2). We get the impression that worship was a lifestyle for the leaders in the church at Antioch. Worship brings joy to the heart of God and delight, comfort, energy, and healing to the heart of the worshippers. It gradually introduces us to more and more of God's glory and leaves us passionate to see him worshipped in all the earth. Nothing less is acceptable. It deepens

> *Worship brings joy to the heart of God and delight, comfort, energy, and healing to the heart of the worshippers.*

our intimacy with him and conditions us to feel more of his heart. It prepares us to hear him when he is ready to speak and to hear him more accurately. It demonstrates to him that we love being with him even when we do not hear him speaking.

There is spiritual authority in worship. It creates space for God. He inhabits the praises of his people. Worship drives back spiritual forces arrayed against Christ and his Church, and it creates spiritual space for new works of God to be born. Worship plays a primary role in kingdom extension.

We discover fasting. "And fasting, . . ." (Acts 13:2). When we look at men and women who have walked with God in the Old Testament, the New Testament, and down through Church history, we meet the practice of fasting. It is pervasive among those who have known God intimately.

Fasting is an outer expression of an inner decision to hunger after God and learn his ways. It is a practical aid that brings clarity and focus to the soul. It muffles other voices and distracting impulses. It softens the heart and humbles the spirit before the Creator.

Hearing God is a process. It is not that God is playing hard to get. In order to hear and correctly interpret what he has to say, we must listen and focus. God is eager to speak, but he seldom wastes words on unhearing or distracted ears.

Fasting is representative of a cluster of activities that have been known and practiced since Old Testament times by individuals in pursuit of God. These have been called spiritual disciplines. Jesus practiced and taught them. Examples include solitude, silence, fasting, chastity, study, worship, prayer, and fellowship. They have absolutely no merit in and of themselves. But, when practiced freely and graciously with the right understanding and motives, they have power to train the inner person in the ways of God.

Absolutely nothing is more critical to the completion of God's purpose on earth than the formation of the inner person before God. No human enthusiasm, will power, or strategy can

> *Absolutely nothing is more critical to the completion of God's purpose on earth than the formation of the inner person before God.*

substitute. Think for a moment—we leaders have sent thousands into the world with the gospel who have returned wounded, disillusioned, and defeated. Many were unprepared in the inner person. Let's not do that anymore. It is not God's design.

We discover the Holy Spirit. "The Holy Spirit said, . . ." (Acts 13:2). God's strategy for Paul did not come from a planning session. It came from the Holy Spirit who spoke to God's leaders as they worshipped and fasted.

This is not at all to dishonor the process of planning. Planning, in its proper place, is responsible activity. It shows trustworthiness. It brings human experience, knowledge, and wisdom to bear in appropriate ways in carrying out God's work. It has many biblical applications. God works in partnership with humans.

But human planning must find its proper place and order. It doesn't come first. God comes first. It is his call, his instructions, his confirmation, his timing, and his empowering. This is his work. It is so natural for us to turn first to our own ideas, wisdom, and convictions as to how things ought to be done! Then we ask God to bless them.

God speaks to those who wait and listen. Waiting and listening come first, mingled generously with patience. God's voice comes next. Once God has finished saying what he has to say, the God-given human capacity to plan can kick in, not before. God sets the parameters. Human beings—prayerfully, sensitively, and humbly—fill in the blanks.

Once human plans are set, God retains the right to override them. Paul and his team had this experience with their plans to preach the Word in the province of Asia. The Holy Spirit prevented them. They then planned to go to Bithynia. The Holy Spirit would not allow them. Then he led them to Macedonia. The gospel entered Europe. Much fruit ensued (Acts 16:6–10).

The Holy Spirit is everywhere present. God's kingdom is at first unseen, although the more it expands, the more it is manifested in the visible world. Advancing this kingdom is a process of living connected with and directed by the Holy Spirit.

We discover being set apart. "Set apart for me" (Acts 13:2). One of the most important issues relating to a local church launching church plants among unreached peoples is the relationship between the apostolic leader and team and the church. This relationship can become awkward and stress filled. Why?

One obvious factor is immaturity in character. Apostolic leaders, while they are still maturing, can be self-willed, prideful, and non-submissive. On the other hand, church leaders can be authoritative, controlling, and narrow-minded. This creates problems.

Another reason the relationship can become awkward is that local churches often have leaders who are gifted in very different ways from leaders who are gifted apostolically. Gifts of teaching, pastoring, and administrating may predominate. It is crucial that each leader understands his or her own gifting, the gifting of other leaders with whom he or she relates, and how they complement each other. This complementing must be lived out in love, esteeming one another better than oneself (Phil. 2:3). Church leaders may be unsure how to relate with and release leaders among those who are called and gifted by God to initiate new works.

A third reason is that leaders in a local church often feel different motivations and priorities than apostolic-type leaders.

Church leaders

- are motivated to nurture the saints.
- are focused on stability.
- invest in building consensus.
- have schedules already full to overflowing.
- tend to avoid risks.
- work for gradual change.

Apostolic leaders

- are motivated to initiate new works.
- are focused on change.

- invest in blazing a trail for others to follow.
- are often chafing at the bit to get on with the new vision.
- tend to embrace risks.
- ask God for dynamic breakthroughs.

It is so valuable for the apostolic leader to spend time ministering in the local church. It will grace him with understanding in many crucial areas.

A fourth reason is that those of us who cherish a high view of the local church can underestimate the role and importance of the apostolic structure. By *apostolic structure,* we mean the organizational form that supports and facilitates apostolic outreach. We could also use the terms *parachurch organization, mission agency, sodality,* etc. Apostolic ministry is released through apostolic structures. We will look at this concept in more depth in Chapter 12, Apostolic Release. When an appropriate structure is not in place, apostolic ministry and its leaders will be frustrated.

> *Apostolic ministry is released through apostolic structures.*

Before Acts 13:1–3, Paul and Barnabas were ministering within the structure of the local fellowship. We might think of them as being members of the church or even on staff.

But that relationship was about to change. They were to be "set apart." What does that mean? It means they were leaving. What were they leaving? They were leaving their old work (ministry) of teaching great numbers of people in Antioch. Why? It was time for them to be released into the new work to which God had called them, to carry his name before the Gentiles. This new work could not be done in the church at Antioch. It was beyond the church at Antioch. It was a different kind of ministry that required a different kind of structure. From then on, they were the members or staff of an apostolic team.

There is more for us to say about apostolic structures. We will explore this matter further in a following chapter.

We discover a team. *"Barnabas and Saul"* (Acts 13:2). Again, it is crucial to establish that God's design for Paul, this groundbreaking, trend-setting, initiating apostolic leader, was to serve in the context of a team. The team formed and served as the apostolic structure.

We discover a work. *"For the work to which I have called them"* (Acts 13:2). The work to which God called Paul was "to carry my name before the Gentiles and their kings and before the people of Israel" (Acts 9:15). The end results of Paul's efforts were churches (Acts 14:23). In today's terminology, the work to which Paul was called was church planting among unreached peoples.

We discover prayer. *"So after they had fasted and prayed"* (Acts 13:3). Prayer is mentioned subsequent to the group hearing God's direction to set apart Barnabas and Paul for the work. Why was more prayer needed?

It is one thing to know that we have heard God. It is another

> *In today's terminology, the work to which Paul was called was church planting among unreached peoples.*

to have heard him accurately. How easily our human imperfections can distort what he has said. Wise is the person and the group who invests time in God's presence, waiting for God's confirmation of what he has said.

God's general direction had been given. And that raised many further questions: How should God's instructions concerning Barnabas and Saul be communicated to the rest of the church? What would be the actual date of the team's departure? Where should they go first? What should they take along? What should their strategy be for preaching the gospel? How should communication with the church in Antioch be set up? Should they return? When? Should others go with them?

Carrying the name of the God of Israel before the Gentiles and their kings and before the people of Israel must have sounded intimidating. This was no easy assignment! The Gentiles had their own gods and Israel had its own entrenched views, often unbiblical, of what God required. This work would require powerful anointing. We can imagine much time and energy invested in prayer before the team went out.

We discover the laying on of hands. "They placed their hands on them" (Acts 13:3). Today when church leaders lay hands on someone for the same purpose they did here, we call it ordination. Those who do the ordaining recognize God's call on the individual for a specific ministry role and are publicly identifying themselves with the person and his or her ministry. There is a sense of shared responsibility between those doing the ordaining and the person being ordained.

Whose responsibility is it to see the nations blessed? Each person is to fulfill the role God has chosen for him or her. It is far too common for mission teams to go among the unreached without the broadly shared participation the mission requires for success. When a sense of ownership of the team and the work is cultivated among the church, the mission has a much higher possibility of producing fruit.

Summary of Recommended Components
for Mission Initiatives

The church. Intentionally root mission initiatives in the life of Jesus as it is resident in local Christian communities (churches). Let the initiative come forth from this base.

The ministry roles of Ephesians 4:11–13. Select leadership for the initiative that is apostolic in nature, and give that leadership the appropriate freedom to form and lead the initiative.

Worship. Ensure that vital worship is part of the lifestyle of all participants. External programs, no matter how much they have to recommend them, void of spiritual power will not result in kingdom breakthroughs.

Fasting. Learn and teach the biblical process of spiritual formation of the inner person in the character of Christ. Develop a mature use of spiritual disciplines, including fasting.

The Holy Spirit. Intentionally and unhurriedly seek God. Look for and depend upon the leading of the Holy Spirit—his call, direction, timing, leaders, and instruction—before proceeding. Remain responsive to his course corrections.

Setting apart. Identify or establish the apostolic structure through which the apostolic initiative is to be carried out. Ensure that the people who minister in the apostolic structure are authentically integrated into the fellowship of a local church.

Team. Carry out all of the functions of the initiative in teams.

The work. Expect the Holy Spirit to lead so that the work is relevant and strategic in light of the present world situation and the progress of world evangelization. How is the work connected to establishing God's rule among unreached peoples?

Prayer. Ensure that all activities are generously permeated with prayer.

Laying on of hands. Invest the energy required to cultivate a meaningful level of ownership of the mission and team throughout the church fellowship.

**There is no more place for me to work in
these regions. (Rom. 15:23)**

*In 1 Corinthians 12:28, we find an intriguing
statement about apostolic ministry: "And in the church
God has appointed first of all apostles." What does
this mean? In what sense are apostles first? Lest we
think they are to be above everybody else, Paul has
already instructed us in the same letter, "For it seems
to me that God has put us apostles on display at the
end of the procession" (1 Cor. 4:9). In one sense,
apostles are first. In another sense, they are last.*

*My understanding is that God has designed
apostolic leaders to go first in sequence. They are to
blaze the trail, to pioneer, to initiate kingdom breakthroughs into new areas, and to lay foundations on
which others can build. When it comes to extending
the reign of God on earth, they have to go first.*

*If this is true, it makes it pretty important to know
who they are. How can we identify them? What characteristics does the New Testament assign to those
who carry this designation? In developing younger
people, how can we look for those who may have this
calling and gift?*

CHAPTER 9

Identifying Apostolic Leaders

F airly early in my missionary experience, the Lord strongly instructed me, through the words of 2 Timothy 2:24, saying, "And the Lord's servant must not quarrel; instead, he must be kind to everyone." I remember times when I have quarreled with my brothers and sisters over points of doctrine. I am so sorry for having done that. It did not honor my Lord or further his purposes. I never want to do that again.

In the last chapter, I mentioned that I am very aware that significant portions of the Church today hold the view that the ministry of the apostles ceased with the death of the twelve. I have deep respect for the churches and their leaders who carry this conviction, but must we all have the same understanding of apostolic ministry? I don't think so. Should different views prevent us from sharing loving fellowship and fruitful service? I don't believe they should. Let's walk this road together, learning from the Lord and from one another. I know that I need and desire much more understanding here. As God's people sincerely grappling with the question, How do we complete world evangelization? let's treat each other in the spirit of Philippians 2:3: "In humility consider others better than yourselves." Being Christ-like is more important than being "right."

> *Being Christ-like is more important than being "right."*

Words are important. They carry concepts. Concepts need to be clearly and accurately defined. What a word means to one person can be very different from what it means to another. This is no doubt true of the word *apostle*.

The word *apostle* might trigger more concern in some than the word *apostolic* or even the compound *apostolic-type*. Notice the difference between saying, "He is an apostle," "He is an apostolic leader," or, "He is an apostolic-type leader." Similarly we can speak of apostolic ministry or even apostolic-type ministry. If we have hesitations about the role of the apostle today, using the adjective might give us more freedom to talk openly about this subject.

Where do we go from here? First, let's seek to allow the New Testament to define apostolic leaders for us. What distinguished them from others? That is the focus of this chapter. Then, in subsequent chapters, it will be important to examine what the New Testament teaches us about the character of apostolic leaders and to begin to explore the process of developing and releasing them.

New Testament Characteristics of Apostolic Leaders

Apostolic leaders are called by God. "Paul, an apostle— sent not from men nor by man, but by Jesus Christ and God the Father" (Gal. 1:1).

Apostolic leaders are called by God to initiate kingdom advances. It is lonely work. Other people, even Christians, will often not understand what motivates them. Satan will oppose. There will be deep valleys. There will be times when God's apostolic leader will say, "Father, I don't want this. I didn't ask for this. This is too hard. I want out."

Jesus reached this place in the Garden of Gethsemane. "'Father, if you are willing, take this cup from me; yet not my will, but yours be done.' An angel from heaven appeared to him and strengthened him" (Luke 22:42–43). At times like this, on a level in his own soul that is deeper than his pain, God's leader will remember experiences with God that he simply cannot deny. He will know that God has led him to do this.

Apostolic leaders are sent by God. "Again Jesus said, '... As the Father has sent me, I am sending you.' And with that he breathed on them and said, 'Receive the Holy Spirit'" (John 20:21–22).

The Greek work *apostolos*, translated *apostle*, means literally "one sent forth." It can carry the meaning of someone sent on a special assignment, like an ambassador, or someone sent with an important message, representing the one who sent him. As we contemplate the word *apostle*, we feel movement, delegated authority, and the risks inherent in carrying a lot of responsibility in unfamiliar and even unfriendly circumstances.

> As we contemplate the word apostle, we feel movement, delegated authority, and the risks inherent in carrying a lot of responsibility in unfamiliar and even unfriendly circumstances.

In God's design, he gave the church in Antioch a beautiful, grace-filled role in the sending out of Barnabas and Saul. But, as though to make sure we do not miss a crucial point, the Holy Spirit added in Acts 13:4, "The two of them, sent on their way by the Holy Spirit."

Apostolic leaders are entrusted by God with a specific area of influence. "They saw that I had been entrusted with the task of preaching the gospel to the Gentiles, just as Peter had been to the Jews" (Gal. 2:7).

Paul and Peter had been given different assignments. Some are called to a certain geographic area, others to a specific cultural or social group, and still others to the business, professional, or academic worlds. It is important for the apostolic leader to discern and honor the arena to which God has sent him.

Two hours before writing these words, I heard about a group

of Christian businessmen committed to extending God's kingdom internationally. Their calling is to do this from within the business world. They have initiated various business enterprises for the purpose of funding mission initiatives, and they have established an impressive track record in doing so. They have just taken a month to seek the Lord for future direction. The leadership roles they are playing in the advance of the gospel speak to me of apostolic calling and gifting that is being expressed in the marketplace. I encounter a growing number of examples like this. Such business people should rightly be honored for their service to Christ and his church. They are as crucial as anyone else in the ongoing advance of the gospel.

The focus of this book is completing Christ's purpose among all nations. We looked at the role of apostolic leaders in the context of unreached peoples, but it is certainly true that this calling is operating in cultures where the church is already established.

Apostolic leaders are gifted by God for the role that he has called them to. "Now about spiritual gifts, brothers, I do not want you to be ignorant...And in the church God has appointed...apostles " (1 Cor. 12:1, 28).

Initiating new works of God is a spiritual undertaking. It calls for a deep knowledge of God and his ways. It is also demanding. It requires a wide range of skills. It is dependent on God's gifting.

What might be the relationship between terms like *calling*, *gifting*, *character*, *anointing* and *mature ministry* in the realm of apostolic ministry or other ministry areas? Let me offer some working definitions. I don't mean for these to be rigid, but I find them to be a helpful framework when working with individuals and churches. They are to be used loosely, with a lot of flexibility and grace. We stand on holy ground here. Only God has the exact specifications:

Calling is, in the first instance, God summoning a person to play a specific role in the work of his kingdom. Once the person matures into that role, the role itself becomes his or her calling. The unique calling God has chosen for each individual is the most gracious, wise, and fulfilling experience imaginable for that person. *Gifting* is the capacity, given to us by the Holy Spirit, which is required to fulfill God's calling. God never calls us to do something he does not gift us to do. I am using the term *gifting* in a broad sense to include natural abilities and learned skills, all of which are gifts of God's grace to us.

When working with individual people, I can't, in every situation, differentiate precisely between spiritual gifts, natural abilities, God-given personality traits, and learned skills. In some instances the lines of demarcation seem very clear. In others, all seem to work together in one unique, indivisible, irreplaceable person.

In the apostolic leader, this gifting will often surface early. Sadly, gifting does not always mature into fully effective ministry. The heart choices of the individual who carries it are crucial because they form character. God's gifting can only be expressed effectively when it is rooted in and nurtured by godly character.

> *God never calls us to do something he does not gift us to do.*

Character as we are using it here refers to godly character. It is Christ-likeness in the inner person. This too is the work of the Holy Spirit, but it is always in harmony with, and never in violation of, heart decisions made by the person. God forms Christ in us through choices and practices that we embrace.[5]

Anointing is empowering by the Holy Spirit for ministry. Character is God's work *in* us. The process of its formation is largely unseen. Anointing is God's hand *upon* us. Its presence is clearly seen by the spiritually sensitive and mature person.

Mature ministry is the expression of a person's calling and gifting, rooted in and nurtured by Christ-like character, and empowered by God's anointing upon the person. When it comes to the apostolic leader, we could express it this way: Apostolic calling and gifting *plus* Christ-like character *plus* God's anointing *plus* God's circumstances and timing *equals* mature apostolic ministry.

Apostolic leaders carry vision given to them by God. "After Paul had seen the vision, we got ready at once to leave for Macedonia, concluding that God had called us to preach the gospel to them" (Acts 16:10).

> *Apostolic calling and gifting + Christ-like character + God's anointing + God's circumstances and timing = mature apostolic ministry.*

This is not the same thing we refer to in secular life as being a visionary leader. The vision does not come from the personality or social context of the leader. It is vision given by God for his purposes. It might, in fact, be contrary to the personality of the leader or his social context.

Initiating leaders see things, and they often see them long before others do. At first they can seem out of step with the majority around them. More practical minds may receive the vision as unrealistic, even irresponsible. But when it has come from God, he will bring it to fulfillment in his time.

Vision from God comes initially in the invisible realm. It must be received there by faith. There it is also tested, sometimes severely. The one who has received the vision will have to wait in faith, holding the vision in the invisible realm, sometimes for years.

As God honors his vision and the person who has faithfully carried it, the vision becomes more and more tangible. The more the vision is transferred into physical reality, the more people understand, own, and celebrate it. Not every vision is from God. And every vision from him will be tested, refined, and matured. A vision may cost the leader everything, but it will also yield spiritual treasures beyond description.

I first saw a vision of global mission coming from a Christian community while the ship *Doulos* was visiting Rosario, Argentina, in July 1979. It was our first visit to Latin America. The scene is still indelibly etched in my memory. We had pleasant surroundings for a berth. You came down the ship's gangway and walked across a green park to the city center that lay just beyond.

One day I was walking along the riverbank, seeking God about the future. We now had two ships, and an expanding team of us had invested many intensive years serving God together. The testing we had weathered together had made our personal bonds very deep. What God had given us in shared experiences and in each other was far too precious to lose. But I knew people could not remain forever on the ships. What was the way forward?

As I was praying, I saw a picture of a group of people. I don't know how many—maybe several hundred. They were worshipping together. They were praying together. Their shared life in Christ formed a spiritual center that glowed like embers at the core of a bonfire. People were being drawn into this core for ministry and healing. And people were being sent out into all the world with the gospel.

That picture has never left me. It found its first expression in the founding of OM Ships headquarters in Mosbach, Germany. That headquarters is more than just an operational base. It is a community of people providing a home for a worldwide outreach. The vision found its next expression in the forming of Antioch Network. This vision has brought me the severest tests of my life—tests that have brought me to utter despair on more than one occasion. But those are other stories for other times.

Apostolic leaders see the big picture. "But now that there is no more place for me to work in these regions, and since I have been longing for many years to see you [in Rome], I plan to do so when I go to Spain....Now, however, I am on my way to Jerusalem....For Macedonia and Achaia were pleased to make a contribution*"* (Rom. 15:23–26).

How many believers find it a challenge to think beyond their neighborhood? Look at the breadth of this man's vision! Paul's "neighborhood" stretched from Israel to Spain. It all felt like his territory to him. Relevant, strategic vision begins with the big picture. It works from the general to the specific. It sees the basic

> *Relevant, strategic vision begins with the big picture. It works from the general to the specific.*

issues that must be addressed. It is in touch with its environment and the trends within it.

This is so relevant to forming mission strategy. We begin with Christ's "all nations" commission. We next identify nations that have not yet been discipled. We then seek God to hear whether he is leading us to one of these groups. Once we have heard his directions, we are ready to develop strategies.

Big picture visionaries need managers, engineers, and administrators to complete the work they begin. Here is another picture of how vital teams are. But it is crucial that we get the order right. Managers must work for visionaries, not the other way around. Managers can unintentionally stifle leaders if they are senior to them for too long. God's trailblazers must come first once their character has matured to where God can trust them with this role. The consolidators will follow and work with them for God's glory.

Apostolic leaders have faith for things beyond themselves. "Against all hope, Abraham in hope believed and so became the father of many nations, just as it had been said to him, 'So shall your offspring be'" (Rom. 4:18).

Faith is something every believer has. But there is a faith that goes beyond an individual trusting God for his own salvation, personal needs, and circumstances. It is the faith that becomes a channel for kingdom extension and the penetration of the kingdom of darkness (see Heb. 11:32–38). We could call it "initiating faith." It would seem that the apostolic gift, almost by definition, must be accompanied by the gift of faith. This kind of faith translates into a fairly simple and straightforward view of reality:

Since

- There is a God,
- He created all things and has all power, and
- He has promised and is faithful to his promises;

Therefore,

- No matter how impossible something looks or what other people say or think, nothing is impossible for God.

"He faced the fact that his body was as good as dead—since he was about a hundred years old—and that Sarah's womb was also dead. Yet he did not waver through unbelief regarding the promise of God, but was strengthened in his faith and gave glory to God, being fully persuaded that God has power to do what he had promised" (Rom. 4:19–21).

Apostolic leaders initiate new works of God. "But now that there is no more place for me to work in these regions" (Rom. 15:23).

Leaders who carry a strong pastoral gifting take a lot longer to get to this place, if they ever do. I can just hear one of them saying to Paul, "Nowhere else to work? Look at the needs all around us! Marriages are under attack. Believers are struggling with addictive behaviors from their former lives. Even our church leaders are experiencing stress in their relationships. There is more work to do here than we could do in several lifetimes."

But Paul would have looked at these same issues from a different perspective—the perspective of his calling and gifting. He had entered the territory, proclaimed the gospel, seen people respond, laid the foundations, and raised up elders who were now responsible to address these needs. His work as an apostle was done. He was thinking about the needs of those in Rome, in Spain, and in other areas where the church was yet to be established. He was a pioneer, a trailblazer. It was time to move on.

Apostolic leaders lay foundations for these new works. "By the grace God has given me, I laid a foundation as an expert builder, and someone else is building on it" (1 Cor. 3:10).

Every time a new work of God is formed, foundations are laid.

> *The God-given ability to lay foundations carries the ability to repair them.*

These foundations must be laid upon the original foundation of the church laid by Christ and the New Testament apostles and prophets (1 Cor. 3:11, Eph. 2:20). The God-given ability to lay foundations carries the ability to repair them.

Apostolic leaders identify, develop, and establish new leaders for these new works. "Paul and Barnabas appointed elders for them in each church" (Acts 14:23).

Here is a crucial element in pioneering ministry: unless new leaders are developed and put in place, the process of initiating new works will quickly come to a halt. What has been initiated will implode.

This calls for seasoned maturity in the apostolic leader. It tests and reveals character. Moving on to the next challenge often appears more appealing than nurturing the current work to self-sustainability. This requires faith, patience, humility, and, above all else, love. The next generation of leaders must be in place and prepared for the heavy responsibility they will carry. If a leader has not demonstrated that he can raise up the next generation of leaders, he is not ready to continue initiating.

When a work is beginning, there is a season of excitement. There are new people, a new facility, and a new environment. Even having to improvise in lots of areas can be fun—for a while. Then what used to be exciting gets to be routine, and eventually unappealing. Relationships go deeper and begin to be tested. Criticism surfaces. Neighbors misunderstand. People in whom we have invested the most become angry and bitter. (As has been said, "Sheep bite!") Potential leaders we are depending on prove to be untrustworthy. And we think, "Let's go somewhere else and start over."

I was meeting recently with a seasoned Latin American church planter. God had used him to start four churches, all of which are doing well, at least on the outside. He has a strong team working with him. Invitations are coming from other needy areas, asking for him to come and start new churches. As we discussed this, he made it clear that at this point he did not feel free to start new works. Two of the four churches were still dependent on him and his team for their leadership and stability. To start a new work would stretch them all too thin and jeopardize what had already been initiated and was still immature. This is the sign of a mature apostolic leader.

Apostolic leaders are often sought to provide apostolic ministry to works they were not involved in starting. "I planned many times to come to you (but have been prevented from doing so until now) in order that I might have a harvest among you, just as I have had among the other Gentiles" (Rom. 1:13).

For a host of reasons, it is often the case that churches and other works of God do not have apostolic leaders available to them. They suffer under this lack, just as they would if a pastoral or teaching ministry were unavailable. The full design of Christ for his Church is not present. More and more these churches and other works are recognizing this need and approaching those who are gifted with apostolic-type ministry. As powerful relationships of trust and service are cultivated, the life-giving ministry of the apostle can nourish and strengthen these works.

I remember the first time a church approached me specifically in these terms. I had known the church and senior pastor for many years. They had been active participants in Antioch Network. They carried a beautiful heart for church planting among unreached peoples and to expand God's kingdom in their local area. I had ministered among them a number of times. This was one of the many churches among whom, whenever I was with them, it felt like coming home again.

But there were dimensions in which the church and its leadership were not bearing the fruit they desired. They came to realize that they had leadership and oversight needs that their leaders or congregation members could not meet. They approached another leader and myself, asking us to serve them in an apostolic oversight role, and asked another brother, called and graced of the Lord, to serve them in prophetic ministry.

The three of us now meet with the church and its leadership periodically. At each meeting, there is the sense of God's graciousness working to impart his wisdom through us. We leave them stronger than they were when we arrived. This is all God's grace, carried out in the context of trusting relationships. There is no authoritarian role here, except the kind of authority that comes when others recognize God's calling and gifting upon another and submit to the benefits thereof.

I find many younger church leaders looking for more experienced leaders to whom they can turn in the challenges and unknowns they face. One morning at breakfast with a younger senior pastor, two-thirds of the way through our time together, he paused and slowly asked, "You know, George, I do not have a spiritual father in my life. Is Antioch Network a place where I could find that?"

Apostolic leaders have strong personalities that enable them to overcome huge obstacles. "I have worked much harder, been in prison more frequently, been flogged more severely, and been exposed to death again and again" (2 Cor. 11:23).

Remember, these leaders are designed by God to penetrate the kingdom of darkness. They lead the frontal attack and establish the beachhead. Think of the strongholds Satan has over individuals, families, neighborhoods, cultures, and countries. God is in the business of tearing down these strongholds, and apostolic leaders are the ones he has chosen to lead the way. They need to be strong personalities!

It is precisely because they are strong personalities that character maturity is such a crucial issue. Leaders with strong personalities who lack humility, patience, sensitivity, and love can do real damage to themselves and others. But it is incredibly powerful when they are able to work together. The process matures them more deeply in the attributes of Jesus, and these attributes are in turn lived out in the midst of those they lead.

> *Think of the strongholds Satan has over individuals, families, neighborhoods, cultures, and countries. God is in the business of tearing down these strongholds, and apostolic leaders are the ones he has chosen to lead the way.*

Apostolic leaders are tested. "This is my gospel, for which I am suffering even to the point of being chained like a criminal. But God's word is not chained. Therefore I endure everything for the sake of the elect" (2 Tim. 2:8–10).

Their calling is tested. The vision is tested. Some co-workers they have relied on prove unfaithful. Satan's opposition is relentless. Testing even comes from their own unwise and immature decisions, and they must often carry the painful consequences for years. In the midst of it all, God's grace is greater, his forgiveness sweeter, and the spiritual benefits of suffering in faith and love more wonderful.

Antioch Network began unintentionally. In 1987 we invited a number of churches to spend a day together discussing and praying around the idea of our churches launching a church planting initiative to unreached people groups. Subsequent meetings of churches like this came to be known as Gatherings of Churches. The work grew.

In 1994 we convened a Gathering in Los Angeles. It was an

absolute disaster. I remember returning home afterwards. I was in a black hole. I had carried this vision in embryo for fifteen years. I thought that churches would flock to it. They didn't. It was uphill all the way. My colleagues in the mission world thought I had lost my bearings. I had nothing left—no energy, no vision, no faith, no heart.

The only thing I could do for days was retreat into the guest bedroom in our home with my Bible, sit on the floor with my back against the bed, and stare out the window. I was at the end. I had reached a place where all I had was God.

God was enough. He was in that room. He restored me, gradually, tenderly, competently, and at a pace I could endure. He is faithful to his servants. He receives and graces human weakness, even in leaders, perhaps especially in leaders. After all, human weakness is all he really has to work with.

Apostolic leaders carry a keen awareness of personal weakness. "My grace is sufficient for you, for my power is made perfect in weakness" (2 Cor. 12:9).

Severe testing brings God's leader to a place of weakness. This weakness is not feigned. It is very real both to the leader and to those who observe him or her. It is a weakness that cuts to the very root of all ambition, self-confidence, and pride. It is a weakness that fuels the forging of godly humility and genuine spiritual authority.

Apostolic leaders are channels through whom God performs the miraculous. "The things that mark an apostle— signs, wonders and miracles—were done among you with great perseverance" (2 Cor. 12:12).

Proclaiming the kingdom of God involves being an agent for manifesting that kingdom. God's kingdom is a spiritual kingdom. Initially it is invisible. But as God works, the presence and power of his kingdom becomes apparent in physical, material ways. "Thy kingdom come" involves evidence in the physical world that confirms the feeling, "This is the hand of God!"

Apostolic leaders are holy in character. "We work hard

with our own hands. When we are cursed, we bless; when we are persecuted, we endure it; when we are slandered, we answer kindly. Up to this moment we have become the scum of the earth, the refuse of the world" (1 Cor. 4:12–13).

Without holiness in character, we do not have biblical apostolic ministry. Any idea that the two are not inextricably linked is an

> *Without holiness in character, we do not have biblical apostolic ministry.*

offense to the holiness of God and a violation of the highest order of apostolic ministry. We will explore this in more detail in the next chapter.

Apostolic leaders are spiritual fathers. "Even though you have ten thousand guardians in Christ, you do not have many fathers, for in Christ Jesus I became your father through the gospel" (1 Cor. 4:15).

Giving birth to new works of God, and developing leaders for those works, is fatherly activity. It is one of God's leaders' greatest rewards. It is foundational to the human condition to need fathering. The need among the saints is pervasive.

Can women be called and gifted by God to serve in an apostolic role? It is my understanding that no New Testament spiritual gift is gender specific. Any spiritual gift, given by God, as character matures, will be expressed. Apostolic gifting will ultimately express itself in apostolic ministry. In Romans 16:7, Paul introduces us to Junias, a feminine name, and designates her as "outstanding among the apostles." An excellent book that provides careful teaching on the role of women in the work of God is *Why Not Women: A Biblical Study of Women in Missions, Ministry, and Leadership* by Loren Cunningham and David Joel Hamilton.

Identifying Potential Apostolic Leaders

If God provides apostolic leaders for the purpose of extending of his kingdom, we can be certain he places them among us. How can we know who they are? What do they look like in our context? For many, the term *apostle* or *apostolic leader* conjures up images of a very unusual person. That might set us off in the wrong direction. Think for a moment of how much initiating energy is still needed to fill the earth "with the knowledge of the glory of the Lord as the waters cover the sea" (Hab. 2:14). We need to initiate among the nations, within our own countries, cities, neighborhoods, and churches. Let's anticipate that there are far more of these called-and-gifted-by-God leaders than we might initially imagine.

There is holy mystery in God's ways of choosing, gifting, and empowering people. Precise formulas can't capture the essence. But there are indications we can watch for, especially in younger leaders and potential leaders. These indications do not prove that spiritual gifting is present, but older leaders would do well to observe carefully those who display these traits.

I was recently invited to minister among a group of churches who excel in this area. Having started with a single church, they have now planted a couple dozen congregations in their city and have sent church planters to other parts of the country and to other countries. How did they do it?

Whenever I am there, I am aware of being surrounded by developing leaders. Younger leaders are being attracted like bees to honey. The older leaders watch for signs of leadership in younger men and women. When they see it, they encourage it and give it a place to express itself within appropriate safeguards. Younger leaders are thoroughly discipled. Then, as they prove themselves, they are freed to broader levels of leadership and mentored by more seasoned leaders. In time, new works are born.

A note to senior pastors and church leaders: Many of these folks are in our churches! We will get the first chance to discern God's purpose for them and to enter into the fulfilling role of contributing to their future development and maturity.

Traits to look for:

- They want to take on new initiatives.
- They have their own ideas of what they want to do.
- They influence people easily and gain a following.
- They do not fit the mold. They color "outside the lines."
- They have a genuine hunger for a deeper relationship with God.
- They show impressive spiritual insight.
- They have noticeable areas of character immaturity.
- They are broad in their horizons and think beyond "our" church.
- They thrive on doing things that are challenging and risky.
- They claim loyalty to "our" church yet seem critical and impatient.
- They tend to become overextended in their commitments.
- We see real potential in them but are unsure how far we can trust them.

Once we identify them, how do we go about developing their capacity and releasing them into the work God has for them? Let's consider that by looking more closely at Paul's process of development. But first, we need to address an issue that is even more crucial.

---

[5]The process of character formation is beyond the scope of this book. Three recommendations for further reading are *The Cost of Discipleship* by Dietrich Bonhoeffer and *The Divine Conspiracy* and *Renovation of the Heart* by Dallas Willard.

Therefore, holy brothers, . . . fix your thoughts on Jesus, the apostle . . . whom we confess. (Heb. 3:1)

In recent years apostle has become for me one of the most beautiful words in the English language. That is why it hurts so much to hear it misused. We have seen that one function of the New Testament apostle was to repair foundations. These days it feels like our understanding of apostle needs some repair.

Where are repairs needed? A critical area is our view of the character of apostolic leaders. Apostolic leaders have been entrusted with such an important role in the design of God's kingdom that a corresponding depth of godly character is absolutely essential for this role to be carried out responsibly and fruitfully. Character was central to all that was taught and modeled by Jesus, Paul, and others who carried this designation in the New Testament. How could we miss it? How could we countenance the idea that apostolic ministry can be decoupled from godly character?

Apostolic claims without apostolic character produce apostolic catastrophe.

CHAPTER 10
The Character of
Apostolic Leaders

I do not intend, in emphasizing the role of character in the apostolic leader, to suggest for one moment that Christ-likeness is not God's graciously intended gift for every believer. It most certainly is! We are seeking to address the spoken or unspoken concerns so many of God's people seem to carry—that any idea that apostolic-type ministry has existed throughout church history will release permission for all sorts of ungodly behavior such as arrogance, ambition, greed, lust, domination, etc.

How do we go about describing apostolic character? The New Testament pulsates with it—the life and teachings of Jesus, the life of Paul and the other apostles in Acts, and character passages in the epistles of Paul, Peter, James, John, and Jude. Since Jesus is specifically designated as an apostle in the New Testament, and since we could certainly find no better model to follow, let's look at six character qualities we see in him. We will also look at a passage for each that demonstrates this quality in Paul. Then I would like to close this chapter by referring to a leader in church history, one of a great number, whom I view as having followed Jesus and Paul in this role.

> *Apostolic claims without apostolic character produce apostolic catastrophe.*

Qualities of Apostolic Character in the Ministry of Jesus

The apostolic leader is like Jesus. "Fix your thoughts on Jesus, the apostle and high priest whom we confess" (Heb. 3:1). New Testament authors do not view being like Jesus as something rare or unattainable. On the contrary, it is the norm of the Christian life, the standard. This does not mean we are perfect. At any moment we can and do fail. But it does mean that our Christian walk is characterized by joy, spiritual power, fruitfulness, and victory.

We become like Jesus through being discipled by him. Jesus is the master of how to live in the kingdom of God. Discipleship is being with Jesus, learning from Jesus, and living like Jesus. The idea of actually being like Jesus seems so unattainable in our day because the idea of being discipled by him is so rare.

I repeat that Christ-likeness is God's gracious intention for every believer. And Jesus taught us that the more we grow to be like him, the less we are aware that this is true of us. The left hand does not know what the right hand is doing. It is not about achieving the correct external behavior through huge amounts of human effort. It is about the inner person being transformed through his training and the gentle and powerful activity of the Holy Spirit. Thus our outward behavior simply comes to express the Christ-like beauty of the inner person. It is so natural, joyful, and restful. It is like a good tree bearing good fruit.

"Follow my example, as I follow the example of Christ" (1 Cor. 11:1).

The apostolic leader is a servant. "A dispute arose among them as to which was considered to be greatest. Jesus said to them, 'The kings of the Gentiles lord it over them...But you are not to be like that....I am among you as one who serves'" (Luke 22:24–27).

Servanthood is about a heart focus on other people. It is not about ourselves. Apostolic leadership is about God and others, never about the apostolic leader. If it becomes evident that the leader is seeking something for himself or herself through this role, we do not have New Testament apostolic leadership.

It is unacceptable to seek personal advancement, fame, and prosperity in Christian ministry. Personal ambition is "earthly, unspiritual, of the devil." It generates "disorder and every evil practice" among God's people (James 3:14–15). It is not like Jesus.

"Paul, a servant of Christ Jesus, called to be an apostle...(Rom. 1:1).

> *Apostolic leadership is about God and others, never about the apostolic leader. If it becomes evident that the leader is seeking something for himself or herself through this role, we do not have New Testament apostolic leadership.*

The apostolic leader renounces his life. "If anyone would come after me, he must deny himself and take up his cross and follow me. For whoever wants to save his life will lose it, but whoever loses his life for me will find it" (Matt. 16:24–25).

There is a foundational principle of life with God that permeates the biographical accounts of Scripture and church history: hold on to your life and reap what can only be described as death; release your life and reap life that is eternal in length and quality.

The self-denial Jesus spoke of is not asceticism or self-mortification. These are actually filled with self! It is a beautiful yielding, a surrender of faith, a letting go, an exchanging of what is proven to be bankrupt for that which is filled with meaning, joy, fruitfulness, and power. As we grow in the inner person with Jesus to where we increasingly release our life to him, his life flows into us and through us to others. This is at the core of Christian ministry. We become channels of his life and grace. Death works in us, and life works in others.

"For we who are alive are always being given over to death for Jesus' sake, so that his life may be revealed in our mortal body. So then, death is at work in us, but life is at work in you" (2 Cor. 7:11–12).

The apostolic leader walks in humility. "Your attitude should be the same as that of Christ Jesus: . . . he humbled himself" (Phil. 2:5, 8).

What does it look like for a leader to walk in humility?

- He does not desire attention for himself. He genuinely wants Christ and others to get the credit.
- He is motivated to serve and to love. He serves by offering others the leadership they need even when it is costly to him.
- He does not defend himself when circumstances put him in a bad light or others criticize. These are God's gifts for his maturing.
- He accepts the losses inherent in his role in submission and faith. He makes room for God to defend him and care for him.
- He is fulfilled when other leaders take over his responsibilities and do them better than he can. It frees him to serve elsewhere.

During the third year of the *Logos*'ship ministry, we visited a country the *Logos* had never been to. As part of our program there, a local committee organized four evenings of evangelistic meetings in an auditorium that seated thousands of people. Since I was the ship director and overall leader, the committee wanted me to be the preacher. They were very concerned that the messages be good.

I wanted to walk in humility, so I insisted that we worked as a leadership team. I also insisted that my colleague, Frank, was a good speaker and that he preach two of the evenings. The committee was skeptical. They wanted me to preach the first and final evenings because it was especially important that they were done wll. But they reluctantly agreed to let Frank preach the second and third evenings.

I preached the first evening. I thought it was a pretty good message, and many people came forward to receive Christ. Frank preached the second and third evenings. On the morning before the fourth meeting, the committee came to me. They wanted Frank to preach that evening. They felt that his preaching was better than mine.

That really hurt! Inside I went through all kinds of emotional gyrations. I had been announced as the final speaker in posters, leaflets, etc. I felt publicly exposed and humiliated. I was the one who insisted that Frank be included as a speaker in the first place—maybe I should have just kept my mouth shut! Frank was very gracious and insisted that I preach. But the more I sorted this through in my heart before the Lord, the more it seemed I began to understand what God was doing. Frank and I had been teaching in many contexts about leadership character. Perhaps God was setting a very public stage for us to live out what we had been talking about.

I went to the final meeting and introduced Frank to the crowd as our final preacher. Since that evening, there have been hundreds of meetings, but what took place inside of me may have been more important in God's kingdom than any message could ever be. That evening I did not reach a state of humility. But through the decision of my heart, in response to circumstances God presented to me, I took one more step down the life-long road of Christ being formed within me.

"For it seems to me that God has put us apostles on display at the end of the procession, like men condemned to die in the arena. We have been made a spectacle to the whole universe, to angels as well as to men. We are fools for Christ" (1 Cor. 4:9–10).

The apostolic leader carries spiritual authority with gracious restraint. "Simon, Simon, Satan has asked to sift you as wheat. But I have prayed for you, Simon, that your faith may not fail. And when you have turned back, strengthen your brothers" (Luke 22:31–32).

How do we picture Paul's authority being exercised among the growing movement of New Testament churches? Many looked to him as their founder, but others (namely the church in Rome) did not. Yet they still recognized his authority and benefited from his ministry.

Some have seen Paul's authority, and that of other apostles, being exercised through organizational-type associations with churches and their leaders. The apostle would issue instructions and carry out discipline similar to the person at the top of an organizational chart.

I view the role of the apostle differently. It corresponds to the role of the loving, sensitive father and mentor. There is real authority, but it is spiritual and relational in nature. Its origin is God's anointing upon the apostolic leader, rooted in godliness of life. It is exercised in love as churches and their leaders seek out the ministry of the apostle and receive it gladly. It is spiritual and relational influence rather than organizational power.

What happens when churches and their leaders will not receive the ministry of the apostle? They must bear the responsibility for their decision before God. This is absolutely central to how God relates to his church. He has created us human and, therefore, free. He honors that freedom, even when it is exercised wrongfully and sinfully. We reap the consequences of our wrong and evil decisions. God hurts with us in the pain that ensues, but he does not violate our freedom.

> *It is exercised in love as churches and their leaders seek out the ministry of the apostle and receive it gladly. It is spiritual and relational influence rather than organizational power.*

I am thinking about a small church that began meeting in homes a number of years ago. There was so much that was good and right and pleasing to the Lord, and it grew. The church started meeting in a school and continued to grow. It was not long before they had their own facility. The growth continued. Eventually Sunday morning attendance passed one thousand and then two thousand. People continued to come.

The pastors and elders found that providing leadership for a larger congregation was far more challenging than it had been when they were smaller. Personal misunderstandings began to emerge within the leadership. There were other challenges the pastors and elders were unsure how to handle. As often happens, the church had grown beyond the experience of its leaders in some crucial areas.

The pastors and elders, motivated by godly wisdom, turned to apostolic leaders in their circle of friendships. They had come to trust these men years earlier. All was not immediately put to rest, and a painful process of working through issues followed. But the church found the help it needed. The pastors and elders grew in their own lives and ministry through the experience. A crucial role was played in the health of the church and the development and mentoring of its leaders by apostolic leaders who were not part of the congregation. The church leaders could trust them.

My own non-scientific survey of the situation in churches today is that this example is more the exception than the rule. Church leaders, in most cases, need more experienced leaders in their circle of whom they turn to when the crises hit. And the crises will come! The enemy is out to destroy the church—nothing new there. And God has made provision. It needs to be accessed.

The essence of spiritual authority is seen when God places his authority upon his minister of proven character. This authority is exercised relationally in love. It has no power to force, only to entreat. When it is dishonored, the offender is committed into the hands of God.

"Therefore, although in Christ I could be bold and order you to do what you ought to do, yet I appeal to you on the basis of love. I then, as Paul—an old man and now also a prisoner of Christ Jesus—I appeal to you for my son Onesimus" (Philem. 8–10).

The apostolic leader models the life of love. "My command is this: Love each other as I have loved you. Greater love has no one than this, that he lay down his life for his friends. You are my friends if you do what I command" (John 15:12–14).

Everything we have written in this chapter is an expression of, and only made possible by, love. "If I have the gift of prophecy and can fathom all mysteries and all knowledge, and if I have a faith that can move mountains, but have not love, I am nothing" (1 Cor. 13:2).

The following four passages from 1 and 2 Corinthians are autobiographical in nature and set character traits in the context of the rigorous demands of apostolic life and service. They contain powerful demonstrations of apostolic character.

> 1 Corinthians 4:9–21   2 Corinthians 6:3–10
> 2 Corinthians 4:7–12   2 Corinthians 11:22–12:10

Let's close this chapter by looking at an apostolic leader from church history. My love for the nations and the church has made the history of Celtic Christianity especially dear and inspirational to me. A strong Celtic church was established in what is now Ireland, beginning in the fifth century, and it overflowed in passion to take the gospel and root the kingdom in what is now Scotland and parts of northern England and continental Europe.

The father of this movement is Patrick (389–461). He was a Briton, originally from what is now England, who spent years in Ireland as a slave. Having escaped and returned to England, God sent him back to Ireland, where he traveled widely, evangelized tirelessly, and founded churches and monasteries throughout the country. He was fearless in his commitment to destroy paganism and to exalt the name of the Triune God. He was a warrior for God in a time and place where fulfilling such a role could be life threatening.

"Patrick's Breastplate" is a statement that has come down through the centuries to us via the Celtic church. We cannot be sure it originated from him, certainly not in the form I am including below. Patrick did not speak the English of today. But the heart and spirit expressed in it have been identified with him for centuries and have inspired generations, including our own. I include a portion of it as a statement that has become a personal treasure, and it serves as a fitting close to a discussion on the character of apostolic leaders.

St. Patrick's Breastplate

I bind myself today
The strong name of the Trinity
By invocation of the same,
The Three in One and One in Three

I bind this day to me forever,
By power of faith, Christ's Incarnation,
His baptism in the Jordan River;
His death on Cross for my salvation;
His bursting from the spiced tomb;
His riding up the heavenly way;
His coming at the day of doom;
I bind unto myself today.

I bind unto myself the power
Of the great love of the Cherubim;
The sweet "Well done" in judgment hour;
The service of the Seraphim,
Confessors' faith, Apostles' word,
The Patriarchs' prayers, the Prophets' scrolls,
All good deeds done unto the Lord,
And purity of virgin souls.

I bind unto myself today
The power of God to hold and lead,

His eye to watch, His might to stay,
His ear to hearken to my need.
The wisdom of my God to teach,
His hand to guide, His shield to ward;
The word of God to give me speech,
His heavenly host to be my guard.

Against all Satan's spells and wiles,
Against false words of heresy,
Against the knowledge that defiles,
Against the heart's idolatry,
Against the wizard's evil craft,
Against the death-wound and the burning,
The choking wave and poisoned shaft,
Protect me, Christ, till Thy returning.

Christ be with me, Christ within me,
Christ behind me, Christ before me,
Christ beside me, Christ to win me,
Christ to comfort and restore me.
Christ beneath me, Christ above me,
Christ in quiet, Christ in danger,
Christ in hearts of all that love me,
Christ in mouth of friend and stranger.

I bind unto myself the name,
The strong name of the Trinity;
By invocation of the same,
The Three in One, and One in Three,
Of whom all nature hath creation;
Eternal Father, Spirit, Word:
Praise to the Lord of my salvation,
Salvation is of Christ the Lord.[6]

[6]Versified from the Irish by C. F. Alexander, *Poems* (London, 1896) pp. 59–62.

**I will show him how much he must suffer for
my name. (Acts 9:16)**

*God is placing apostolic leaders among us. They
are God's leaders. They are in our churches. We might
not recognize them yet, but they are there. They
represent one of God's awesome resources for
impacting our neighborhoods, our cities, and the
nations of the earth with God's kingdom.*

*They also represent a stewardship; we could even
say a challenge. As pastors and church leaders, God
has entrusted us with an important role, perhaps a
even foundational role, in their development. He is the
one who is maturing and preparing them, but, as in
everything he is doing, he is including us as partners.
We are his co-workers in the development of his
leaders.*

*How do we relate to them? It will require insight,
patience, humility, and love. What might the process of
their maturing look like?*

CHAPTER 11

Developing Apostolic Leaders

O nce again, as we seek to understand God's activities with regard to apostolic leaders, the experience of Saul of Tarsus comes front and center. We have so much information in Scripture on the process of his development. By the time he met Jesus on the road to Damascus, God had already made rich deposits in his life. And it was not as though he immediately thereafter went into effectively founding new churches among the nations. Not at all! There was the work of further development still to be done.

In God's process of developing Paul, over decades, for apostolic leadership, what ingredients did he use?

Components in Paul's Development As an Apostolic Leader

Sovereign foundations. In the circumstances of Paul's birth, God positioned him for maximum effectiveness in his call: "This man is my chosen instrument to carry my name before the Gentiles and their kings and before the people of Israel" (Acts 9:15–16).

First, Paul was born a Jew with impeccable Jewish credentials (Phil. 3:4–6). This gave him powerful inroads into Jewish society; he came from their world. Second, Paul was born a Roman citizen in the Greek-speaking world (Acts 22:3). This gave him intimate knowledge of Gentile language and culture; he also came from their world.

Biblical grounding (Acts 22:3). Paul was thoroughly trained by Gamaliel, the most famous Jewish teacher of his time. It is crucial for those who lay foundations in the lives of new believers to be competent in handling the Word of God. This is not to say that everybody must be a graduate of a Bible school or seminary. There is more than one way to become proficient in the Scriptures. But there is no quick or easy way.

The apostolic leader must be able to integrate truths that the Holy Spirit has entrusted to other Christian traditions into his or her biblical understanding. He or she must be able to develop solid biblical grounding on a wide range of matters that will confront any new church with little history in its own culture. Narrowness and theological obtuseness will only yield a foundation that cannot endure the perplexing realities that will confront it.

Life-forming experiences with God (Acts 9:3–9). Regardless of what anybody else said or thought, Paul knew that God had taken the initiative to meet him and that his life's direction was changed by that encounter. Apostolic leaders know they have been with God. A critical component of their maturation is learning to carry that knowledge in humility, faith, and sensitivity without compromise.

> *The apostolic leader must be able to develop solid biblical grounding on a wide range of matters that will confront any new church with little history in its own culture.*

Expect God to bring older, seasoned leaders into their lives as resources to help them process experiences and struggles and to develop their understanding.

Early ministry opportunities (Acts 9:19–20). Almost immediately following his conversion, Paul began to proclaim the gospel. Paul was filled with energy from this encounter. His initial ministry experiences were an immature response to his calling and gifting, but they were essential to his development. Apostolic leaders need plenty of opportunities to engage in ministry early in their development. This is how they learn.

Shortly after I arrived in India as a young missionary, I was honored to receive an invitation to work with Bakht Singh, an apostolic leader who became my first mentor in local church life. He was an inspiration to many of us, and he led a powerful movement of the Spirit that ultimately produced hundreds of churches. I don't want to miscommunicate—that work was not perfect then nor is it now. But they had many things right, and one of them was how they trained leaders. How did they do it?

When a pastor in one of the churches recognized God's hand upon a potential leader, that person would be sent to the home assembly where Bakht Singh was based. There these leaders-in-training would serve in many different areas of church life. Character development was extremely important to them. Trainees would serve in the kitchen, clean the bathrooms, sweep the grounds of the compound, and do whatever needed to be done to serve the wider church fellowship.

Older leaders would observe what gifting God had given these young potential leaders by involving them temporarily in various ministry roles. This was a season of trial and discovery. There were many opportunities: leading early-morning prayer meetings and Bible studies, tract distribution, open-air preaching, personal evangelism and following-up persons who were interested in knowing more of the gospel or who had come to faith.

In this setting the older leaders could recognize the real gifting in a younger leader as it emerged. As such gifting became evident, and as it was coupled with demonstrated Christ-likeness in character, and the maturing of ministry skills, the young leader was given more and more responsibility. Out of this process emerged new church-planters and pastoral leaders.

Introduction to the reality of suffering (Acts 9:23). If we really wanted to recruit people for apostolic ministry, certainly we would not want to speak of suffering. But to avoid this subject would be a denial of Jesus and the Scriptures. He came as the suffering servant, and he called his disciples to suffer. Dietrich Bonhoeffer puts it this way, "When Christ calls a man he bids him come and die."[7] Jesus puts it this way, "If anyone would come after me, he must deny himself and take up his cross and follow me. For whoever wants to save his life will lose it, but whoever loses his life for me will find it" (Matt. 16:24).

Older leaders have an awesome responsibility toward younger leaders. They can share, even transfer, their lives, their hearts, and their faith to them. On the other hand, they can also be a bitter source of their wounding. One way older leaders wound younger leaders is not being fully truthful with them, withholding things from them.

Once Hanna and I visited an area in Central Asia where three church planting teams were working within a four-hour drive of one another. All of them were relatively new arrivals in that part of the world. We were so impressed with these younger people! Motivated by a sincere desire to make Christ known among the unreached, they had gone to that remote area, in some cases with small children, at real personal cost.

As members of two of the teams sought contact with us, however, we increasingly realized how unprepared they were for long-term ministry in that part of the world. They had been recruited to Central Asia in a triumphant climate of mission enthusiasm. Months after they arrived, the reality of what they had taken on began to set in: the cold winters with little heat, the spiritual warfare, the radically unfamiliar culture, the unappealing food, the lack of medical services, the irregularity of electrical and water supply, the loneliness for family and friends back home, and the lack of response from the people.

Neither of those two teams survived. Team members returned home with a sense of personal defeat. What would they say to home churches, prayer partners, and financial supporters? Where was God in all this? Had he really called them? Were they failures? Who and what could they trust?

They had been challenged with mission romanticism but not

been prepared for it. Those who know the reality behind the scenes know that this scenario repeats itself far too often in mission circles.

Those of us who are calling people to mission carry a responsibility to describe the implications clearly and soberly and to do all we can to prepare people as thoroughly as possible. We can't prevent hardship and suffering—they are inseparable from making Christ known among all nations. But we must be truthful and responsible. Jesus spoke clearly about suffering. Church history speaks clearly about suffering. Paul experienced suffering early in his ministry. The kind of suffering he was causing before his conversion became his own experience after it.

The message of Paul's life doesn't end with suffering. It ends with glory. Writing from a Roman prison cell, largely abandoned by those he had depended on, and awaiting martyrdom, Paul wrote, "I have fought the good fight, I have finished the race, I have kept the faith. Now there is in store for me the crown of righteousness, which the Lord, the righteous Judge, will aware to me on that day—and not only to me, but also to all who have longed for his appearing" (2 Tim. 4:7–8).

Desert seasons (Gal. 1:15–24). At various times, God's leaders are ushered into seasons in the desert. These are periods of reduced activity—sometimes voluntary, sometimes not. God often orchestrates such periods for the purpose of deeper inner growth.

Leaders called and gifted to pioneer are strong personalities with significant energy. They tend to be highly motivated for the task. Over time, one of the downsides of this can be the neglect of the inner life. The ability to achieve outwardly can outstrip the maturation of the soul. Godly character is essential to support God's gifting and the fruit it produces. Otherwise, leaders malfunction.

Moses spent the first forty years of his life in Egypt as the son of Pharaoh's daughter. He was surrounded by the best in terms of influence, wealth, education, and unlimited opportunity. At some point he realized that he was a Hebrew. It would seem from the biblical record, although we are not told for certain, that he became aware of God's calling for him to be the promised deliverer. This might explain why he killed the Egyptian he found beating a Hebrew (Ex. 2:1–12). This action is representative of a called-of-God leader beginning to pursue God's calling in his own way and strength. The result is always failure. Moses was banished from Egypt and spent forty years in the desert.

What condition was Moses in when he entered the desert? If we could see what state his soul was in at that point, would we see a parallel with today's "successful" person, driven by a need for outward success to give him or her a feeling of self-worth? How much anger did he have? Was there contempt for others? Lust? Greed? Pride? Hatred? Self-hatred?

What went on in the desert? Here is what I can imagine: God brought Moses face to face with his creator and with his own soul. Moses came to slowly understand the motivations that drove him and were causing his dysfunctions. He learned how to spend time with the God of his fathers, hearing from him, allowing him to heal and change him, and learning his ways. God and Moses became intimate. All this took time—years of quiet before God. God was not in a hurry. He had the time. To take years in the desert forming his servant was well worth it to God.

Moses matured into one of the godliest people who have ever lived. God trusted him with awesome spiritual authority and responsibility, and Moses passed the test, generally, with flying colors. God's assessment of Moses at the end of his life was, "Since then, no prophet has risen in Israel like Moses, whom the LORD knew face to face" (Deut. 34:10). This is the process of the desert. It is the process of becoming intimate with God, of being transformed by God, and being formed into a servant whom God can trust with great responsibility.

Failure is an integral part of the development of an apostolic leader. Periods of reduced activity allow the leader to process areas of failure before God. The leader has reached a wonderful place in his maturation when he realizes that failure is not caused

> *The leader has reached a wonderful place in his maturation when he realizes that failure is not caused by others or even by Satan.*

by others or even by Satan. Satan can oppose and hinder, but he can never win. He is a defeated foe. Failure in our walk with God comes from only one source—our wrong attitudes and choices, in other words, our own character immaturity.

Men and women who have walked with God through the centuries instruct us in the beneficial effects of solitude. We live in a compulsive age that continually tries to mold us into its image. In such a world, there is little time to know God or even our own hearts. We are surrounded by multitudes who have lost contact with their souls.

Solitude breaks the cycle. It gives us space to know ourselves—our thoughts, emotions, motivations, hurts, and intentions. Solitude is healing. It brings focus. It brings us into contact with our own souls. Through it we affirm our humanity. We honor the person God has made us to be, and, in so doing, we honor the Creator.

Paul's experiences in prison are wonderfully instructive here. Why would God allow his apostle to the nations to undergo such long periods of forced inactivity? We gain a glimpse of what God was showing Paul during these times from what Paul wrote while behind bars. And, we see, through his letters to the churches, these seasons of reduced activity turned out to be the most productive and fruitful of his life.

Mentors. God brought more seasoned believers into Paul's life to steer him toward maturity. Ananias was the first example of God showing Paul his need for others (Acts 9:10–18).

Soon Barnabas became a champion and mentor (Acts 9:27; 11:25–26). Later Paul had meaningful contact with Peter and James (Gal. 1:18–19). The other spiritual leaders in the church at Antioch must have also been a source of enrichment and development for him (Acts 13:1).

Apostolic leaders need significant mentors. Their gifting and energies are strong. But during the years (decades) in which wisdom is being honed, this energy can be misapplied, and the results can wound the leader and damage his ministry. Those privileged to mentor God's leaders must have great sensitivity. These leaders can easily feel blocked. From the base of a strong relationship, a mentor needs to steer, guide, and protect without condemning, blocking, or controlling.

Life and ministry in community—the local church. What was Paul doing in his hometown of Tarsus when Barnabas went to get him and bring him to Antioch (Acts 11:25–26)? We have little record of lasting fruit from Paul's ministry during his first eight years as a believer. And that's okay. God was preparing him for the mature years of his life.

What took place while Paul was ministering in the church at Antioch?

- He was maturing in character through living and ministering in the midst of a community of supportive relationships.
- He was learning firsthand the reality of church life. If he was to plant churches, he needed credible church experience.
- He was being grafted into a community where other leaders could confirm his calling and the timing of his release.

Summary: Paul's Development As an Apostolic Leader

Look for individuals. Look for men and women who fit the profile given in the last chapter. They might be candidates for this role. Keep an eye on them. Look for God's confirmation in their development.

Free them to minister early. Establish a role that allows

creative, discretionary choices. Give them as much freedom as is reasonable, but also make it clear, graciously, where their boundaries are. Define lines of communication and accountability. Establish regular times for feedback.

As they minister, address issues that arise. Issues will come to the surface relating to their relationship with God, others, and themselves. Address these issues in the context of a loving, caring relationship. Give them plenty of gracious, respectful affirmation. Be honest where honesty is needed. Define reality where they need it to be defined for them.

There will be suffering. Be available to them during these times. Here is where immaturity can do real damage. Point them to the beautiful life of the resurrection to which Jesus has called us. This suffering has a beneficial purpose that will become more obvious with time.

Link them with mentors. Help them find people they trust who will develop meaningful relationships with them and who can provide regular input into their lives and activities.

If they are not authentically rooted in church life, steer them in that direction. Look for a church whose leaders have demonstrated understanding in developing younger leaders. Teach them why they need this so much. Process with them the inadequacies in the church, which they will see fairly quickly.

As they mature, extend their boundaries. As they prove trustworthy, trust them with more.

Be alert that seasons in the desert will develop. Help them to understand the nature and purpose of such times. Protect them when they need to withdraw from public ministry for a season. They might feel shame in having to communicate the reasons for this. Link them with those gifted in mentoring character formation. Protect the leader from reengaging in activity prematurely.

---

[7]Dietrich Bonhoeffer, *The Cost of Discipleship* (New York: Simon and Schuster,1995) p. 89.

"Set apart for me Barnabas and Saul for the work to which I have called them." (Acts 13:2)

The release of apostolic leaders is a different phenomenon than their development. In practice, there is much overlap. The releasing needs to begin fairly early, long before the development has run its course. Releasing is critical to developing, and developing is never complete.

By release I mean the process that ushers the leader into the mature expression of his or her calling and gifting. The leader's heart enjoys a clear conviction about the ministry role God has chosen for him. This role has been validated through years of experience and affirmed by other mature Christians. Character has developed to where it can support and sustain the fruit produced by strong calling, gifting, and anointing. The leader encounters temptations (like the praises of other people, etc.) without being derailed. We are not talking about perfection. There are ongoing spiritual attacks and inner struggles that repeatedly drive the leader to Jesus. But we are talking about a life characterized by victory. Character has become a reliable source of inner stability and direction that is stronger than external influences.

What does an introduction into such a life-season look like? Paul's experience in the events recorded in Acts 13:1–4, and those surrounding them, give us a much fuller picture of the season of mature release.

CHAPTER 12
Releasing Apostolic Leaders

W e could think of the process of Paul's release as beginning in Acts 9:20, where "At once he began to preach in the synagogues." This has the feel of Paul releasing himself. It was fine as far as it went. We have a new believer following his God-given instincts. But he is not developed or proven in either gifting or character. There is no confirmation by others of his readiness or of God's timing. This is not a fully seasoned condition of release.

We have no record of significant fruit from Paul's ministry during the approximately ten years between his call on the road to Damascus (Acts 9:1–16) and his mature release later (Acts 13:1–4). The call is there, but there seems to be little indication of the powerful anointing of apostolic ministry that we see so clearly from Acts 13 on. Following are six conditions that existed when the Holy Spirit indicated that it was time for Paul's mature release into the work that God had called him to.

Six Qualities Necessary for Apostolic Release

1. Paul's calling and gifting had been expressed and seasoned over years of ministry. The time between God's call on the road to Damascus and Paul's release in Antioch allowed for the development process described in the previous chapter. Paul experienced his strengths and suffered and matured in his weaknesses. He learned the ways of God.

2. Paul's calling *was confirmed by other godly leaders (Acts 13:2).* Someone's assertion that God has called him or her does not ensure that this is the case. God's calling is eventually confirmed in the hearts of other leaders and in the church through the witness of the Holy Spirit. There is often a sense of resonance throughout the local fellowship. "Yes! This feels so right" is the way other people may respond.

One afternoon my telephone rang. On the line was a church leader I greatly respected. He had had a very fruitful ministry on the pastoral staff of his church for a number of years. He was surprised by a feeling he had that God was bringing him to a ministry transition. He was phoning to seek my counsel.

Almost immediately my sense was that, having spent years investing in one church, God was repositioning him so that all he had learned might be made available to many other churches. Obviously, if this were what God was doing, other voices of counsel would have to confirm it, especially in his church. He knew that.

The process of seeking out these voices took many months. Some leaders in his church voiced the inevitable question, "Is it not possible for you to do what God is calling you to do right here?" Good question. As he and his colleagues in the church continued to wait on the Lord, the confirmation grew that God was calling him and his family out.

Hanna and I had the privilege of attending the service when he was sent out. There was some real sadness among the people since he was loved by many. But there was also the sense that they felt it was right. The church was filled with affirmation and blessing for this leader and his family. God had

> *God's calling is eventually confirmed in the hearts of other leaders and in the church through the witness of the Holy Spirit.*

spoken, through the leader, through other leaders, and through the body. It was beautiful.

3. The timing *of Paul's release was confirmed by other godly leaders (Acts 13:2).* The picture here is not one of Paul announcing that he was going to the nations and resenting those who did not jump on board with him right away. The sense is more that although he knew that he had been called by God, he was content to allow him to direct the next step. In an atmosphere of waiting upon God, together with other leaders, the Holy Spirit signaled that the time for his full release had come. The indication was given not only to Paul alone but also to the group of leaders in the church.

The senior pastor of a local church recently spoke with me about a leader in his congregation. This brother is a visionary leader with a strong personality who wants to carry out a particular work among unreached peoples. For a long time, the pastor just could not bless this. The leader was headstrong and did not find it easy to listen to counsel. He and the pastor continually clashed. But things began to change in the pastor's mind when this leader began to show a heart to serve, especially in areas that had nothing to do with mission. More and more the issue became not what he wanted to do but how he could support the church as a whole. He was prepared to serve joyfully behind the scenes.

The pastor has now come to the point where he feels he can bless what this leader wants to do in mission, although he feels the timing is not yet right. The leader has responded well to what his pastor is saying about timing and has embraced waiting on the Lord until his pastor and other leaders feel God's time has come. This story does not yet have an ending, although I believe it will be a beautiful one. Here is a strong leader who has learned to serve and trust God to speak through other spiritual leaders in his life. That is a ripening context for apostolic release.

4. Paul's release came in the context of a local church (Acts 13:1). Paul was not originally from Antioch (Acts 11:25). He was brought there to minister by his champion or mentor Barnabas (Acts 11:26). Paul ministered in the church for an extended time, long enough for him to be authentically grafted into the body (Acts 11:26). This also linked him with other leaders who could serve as his peers, supporters, and protectors. Paul was authentically sent out from the church at Antioch in a way that the church participated meaningfully. Although he returned to Antioch for renewal and refreshment (Acts 14:26–28), there is no indication that the church directed his field decisions (Acts 16:6–10).

5. Paul's release came in the context of a team (Acts 13:4–5). Teams provide a broader diversity of gifting than any individual alone can offer. They can enter into united, believing prayer against the attacks of Satan on the work. They are able to be a supportive mini-community where individual members can receive personal nurture in the midst of their service. They serve as an environment where their members can receive ongoing character development. And healthy teams allow the unbeliever to experience the beauty of Jesus present in the community of believers. Godly team life is a powerful form of evangelism.

I have spoken of the observable reality that women also serve in this calling, and I am thinking of one now as I write. She has been an inspiration to me and many others for years. She has had a strong sense of God's call to the poor most of her adult life, and a fruitful urban ministry has developed around her leadership. This involves meeting tangible needs like food and clothing and also carrying out programs for children from low-income families.

Her reserves of love and energy seem almost limitless, and she can make tons of things happen by herself. For years I have desired for her a larger team of co-workers who could maximize her vision and the opportunities she creates. It is not that she has been against the idea of a team, not at all. It is just that the team has been, until recently, incomplete. The gifts have not been there to supplement her gifts, and the number of workers has been inadequate to implement the scope of her vision.

But over the past two to three years, I have watched God change that. I am thinking of two other leaders whom God has brought alongside her, and, as a result, the ministry has experienced far-reaching advances. One is a leader who has catalyzed the formation of a church that can receive and mature the spiritual fruit of this ministry. A second is an organizational leader who can consolidate, structure, and lay new foundations upon which further growth can be based. Here is an apostolic leader whose calling and ministry are being actualized in greater ways than ever before through the ministry of a team.

> *And healthy teams allow the unbeliever to experience of the beauty of Jesus present in the community of believers.*

6. *The organizational structure that was the vehicle for Paul's release was different than the organizational structure of the local church.* One of the most sensitive issues when mission initiatives come forth from local churches is the ongoing relationship between the church and the mission organization. There can be much misunderstanding here. This does not have to be! The issue warrants our careful, sensitive consideration. The matter is so important that I have chosen to devote a separate chapter to it.

So after they had fasted and prayed, they placed their hands on them and sent them off. (Acts 13:3)

The magnificence of God's design for completing his global mission is only accentuated when we explore the mutual relationship he envisioned churches and mission organizations to enjoy. Each has a God-given capacity to deeply bless and enrich the other. Experiencing the benefits of each other's ministry allows them to grow in their desire to honor and affirm one another, to delight in each other.

Both local churches and mission organizations have been given unique strengths the other lacks and needs. Without mission organizations, apostolic impulses in churches will be inadequately cultivated and ultimately wither. Without local churches, needs within mission organizations for rootedness, resources, and personal care will remain only partially and inadequately addressed.

We see both of these structures in the New Testament. Our modern mission organizations are present-day descendents of the apostolic teams we encounter in the book of Acts. To be sure, there are some noticeable differences between the two. To what degree is some reengineering in order?

CHAPTER 13
Apostolic Organizational Structures

In seeking a biblical understanding of the appropriate relationship between a local church and a mission organization, there are two viewpoints we will want to avoid: The first is that the local church does not need the mission organization. "If the church had been doing its job all along, we would not need mission organizations" is the kind of statement that is heard at times. The second is that the mission organization does not need the local church. "The church should just send us (mission organizations) its people and money and leave the rest of the job to us mission professionals. What does the church know about missions?" would represent this viewpoint.

Neither of these viewpoints is correct or helpful. They are disrespectful to both the local church and the mission organization. They fuel unkindness. They sow seeds of disunity within Christ's body. They do not honor our Lord or advance his kingdom.

In the New Testament, the Holy Spirit provided for the global advance of God's kingdom by forming two structures: local churches and apostolic teams. Most people today would see the modern equivalent of the apostolic team to be the parachurch organization, the mission organization, the sodality, or, sometimes in the United States, the 501(c)(3) non-profit organization.

Paul's apostolic teams were not local churches. And they were also different, in some obvious ways, from our modern mission organizations, especially in the way they have developed over the years. This is not meant to be critical of modern mission organizations or to say that God is not using them. He most certainly is and in awesomely wonderful ways!

> *Paul's apostolic teams were not local churches.*

If we are prepared to consider this matter prayerfully before the Lord, we may find that we want to make adjustments, which would greatly help both churches and mission organizations distribute God's blessings among all nations.

My experience tells me there is growing interest in pursuing this subject. Time and again leaders in mission organizations have asked, "How can we relate more effectively to local churches?" And church leaders have said, "We really want to be proactive when it comes to our mission obedience, but we don't want to reinvent the wheel. How can we work with mission organizations so both of us benefit?" Awesome questions!

Apostolic Structures

Perhaps different terminology would be helpful as we consider these issues. Sometimes new words free us from old images that block us from seeing things with a fresh perspective. The term that has become my favorite in this discussion is *apostolic structure*. The term apostolic structure helps me focus on the core issue: what kind of organizational structure is best suited for the release of apostolic ministry (i.e., the ministry effects apostolic leaders catalyze)?

Since apostolic ministry was a biblical phenomenon, there must have been a biblical structure through which it was released. What was this structure? What

> *The core issue: What kind of organizational structure is best suited for the release of apostolic ministry?*

was its organizational culture? How did it relate to the local church? The biblical structure was the apostolic team. Let's look at this more closely. What were the characteristics of these teams? What implications do these suggest for churches and mission organizations relationships today?

> Apostolic ministry is released through apostolic structures.

Apostolic ministry is released through apostolic structures.

Characteristics of Paul's Apostolic Teams

Paul's apostolic teams were one with the local church. They were seamlessly integrated into the fellowship of believers. They blended in. The church was their family. They had been formed within it. They understood it. They were part of its leadership. They had come from it for the purpose of advancing the kingdom into new areas, or, in other words, to start new churches. And they returned to it.

- Paul and Barnabas were main teachers and leaders in the church at Antioch (Acts 11:25–26; 13:1–3).
- The team of Paul, Barnabas, and John Mark was formed within the church at Antioch (Acts 13:1–5).
- This team was sent out from the church at Antioch.
- Their ministry produced new local churches (Acts 14:23).
- In whatever location they found themselves, the local church was home and family to them (Acts 14:26–28).

My twenty years of serving in highly mobile, cross-cultural ministry were deeply instructive to me in this issue. Both during my years in India and those with the ships *Logos* and *Doulos*, I found myself in a different church most Sundays, often as the speaker.

As a team, we felt a strong sense of unity with and submission to the churches we visited. There were times with the ships when we had a clear idea of the kind of program we wanted to arrange in a particular port city, but local church leaders asked us to adjust it. We always honored their requests. As long as we were in that city, we were part of the body of Christ there. We would never intentionally do our own thing.

While in a port city, we ministered with our brothers and sisters from the churches there. Local believers translated for us in the conferences and evangelistic events. They greeted the visitors to the ship. They served with us in the kitchen, engine room, and other non-public areas. They were part of our prayer meetings and group devotional times. We experienced God together, moving in and through us.

Sometimes hundreds of them came to the quayside just before the ship's departure to say goodbye. It was not unusual for the tugs to be slowly pulling the ship away from the quay while people on the shore and on the ship waved to each other and wept softly. We had been joined together in the work of the kingdom for only two to three weeks, and yet an incredibly powerful bond had been established between us. Doing ministry together tends to do that. We knew indeed that we were one family, one body.

Paul's apostolic teams had an identity separate from the local church. If you went to a gathering of the fellowship on a Sunday, you would have had a hard time pointing out who were Paul's team members. However, during the week, the identity and activities of the team would be clearly distinguishable. And the difference would become even more apparent when the time came, at the Holy Spirit's direction, for the team to leave for another location.

- Paul and Barnabas left the church in Antioch. It was the Holy Spirit who separated them and sent them out (Acts 13:4).
- Paul and Barnabas went to Lystra, Iconium, and Derbe, where they established churches. They subsequently left each of these places, although they later returned for ministry visits (Acts 14:21–22; 15:36).
- Timothy left his church in Lystra to join Paul's team. Church leaders in Lystra and Iconium concurred (Acts 16:1–3).
- Paul left the church at Ephesus, where he had spent three years, apparently never to return (Acts 20:25, 31).

Let's go back to the scene of the ship moving away from the quayside with brothers and sisters on the ship and shore feeling powerfully aware of their oneness in Christ. They were also keenly aware of their differences. The ship team was called of God to move on to the next port city. The local believers were called of God to remain behind to conserve and mature the fruit born in their home city, catalyzed by the ship team. Both of these roles are crucial and of God. How foolish and wrong it would be to compare one unfavorably with the other, as though one is more valid or important than the other. Such attitudes wound the body of Christ.

"I planted the seed, Apollos watered it, but God made it grow. Now neither he who plants nor he who waters is anything, but only God, who makes things grow" (1 Cor. 3:6–7).

Monastic Buildings

In many cases, monastic movements preserved in their buildings a picture of the relationship between the church and the mission structure. From Iona, a small island off the western coast of present day Scotland, Celtic Christians launched a missionary movement in the sixth century that resulted in the evangelization of much of what is today the north of England and parts of continental Europe.

If you visit Iona today, you can see the architectural remains of a design that physically models the structural relationship of the local church and the mission/apostolic ministry. The areas where the monks lived and carried out their ministry are attached to the church building.

What does this arrangement tell us? Those engaged in the apostolic ministry were fully integrated into the fellowship of a local church. They were there when the church assembled. They ministered there. The church fellowship ministered to them. They were an integral part of the church's life. But during the week, they worked in their own arenas and organizational structures, and the church members worked in their arenas, whether as farmer, artisan, or merchant.

With respect to the church, the mission structure allowed for

- Seamless fellowship
- Separate ministry

New Testament apostolic teams were

- One with the local church in relationship
- Different from the local church in purpose

Today, much of our confusion in this area is caused by the fact that we are not clear on the difference between community and structure. The body of Christ in the New Testament was one community with two

> *The body of Christ in the New Testament was one community with two structures.*

structures.

Paul's apostolic teams were called to a different kind of ministry than the local church. God called the apostolic teams to work that was different but fully complementary to the work of the local church. Its components included:

- *Initiation*: Paul and his companions were directed by God to preach the gospel to Europeans for the first time (Acts 16:10).
- *Laying of foundations:* Paul invested himself in establishing the church at Ephesus; from there the whole province of Asia was reached (Acts 20:20; 19:10).
- *Repairing of foundations:* Paul corrected inaccuracies that were generated by another apostle, Peter (Gal. 2:11–13).
- *Oversight*: Paul, along with other team members, exercised gracious, relationship-based oversight of groups of churches (Acts 18:18–23).

Paul's teams were called primarily to kingdom extension, whereas the local church was called primarily to kingdom consolidation. Paul's teams were apostolic in essence, while local churches are pastoral in essence.

These distinctions are not absolute. Apostolic leaders minister pastorally. Apostles—Jesus, Paul, Peter, John, and others— presented all the teaching concerning pastoral ministry in the New Testament. And a local church can be a garden in which the Holy Spirit plants apostolic calling. This is a core message of this book!

But we all can't do everything with equal intensity. The body of Christ is diverse. Our individual callings and giftings are diverse. This is God's magnificent design.

Paul's apostolic teams were a different kind of organizational structure than a local church.

- They made their own decisions, led by the Holy Spirit, regarding what their movements and tasks were to be (Acts 16:6–10).
- They were responsible for their own funding. They worked at trades and received gifts (Phil. 4:14–19).
- They did their own recruiting, in collaboration with the appropriate church leaders (Acts 16:1–3).
- They operated in a broad and diverse geographic area (2 Tim. 4:9–13).

The motivation behind local church organization is primarily to nurture and provide stability for the members. The apostolic motivation is to create organizational structures for the purpose of accomplishing tasks, particularly ones that take place in far-away locations and are focused beyond the life and perspective of the home community. Paul's apostolic teams enjoyed strong relational ties with the church in Antioch, which released them. But in some ways they had a distinct ethos and structure:

The church at Antioch	Paul's team
Designed to be stationary	Designed to be mobile
Focused on local issues	Focused on cross-cultural issues
Valued stability	Valued advance, even if risky
Wanted to grow where it was	Wanted to go to new locations
Financed by its members	Responsible for its own finance
Led by God through its leaders	Led by God through its leaders
Linked with the team spiritually	Linked with the church spiritually

Although we are looking at two kinds of structures, we see no hint in the New Testament that they felt anything but affirmation and support for each other. They were equal, mutually valued partners in the work of Christ's kingdom. The church at Antioch found that most of its energies were absorbed in the local work. It rejoiced that there were leaders like Paul and Barnabas, who were called and gifted by God to extend the kingdom among the Gentiles. And Paul and his team, likewise, were deeply thankful for the pastoral leaders in Antioch, whose faithful ministry freed them to pioneer the kingdom in new areas.

Implications for Local Churches Today

As a local church discovers the Holy Spirit moving them toward a strategic focus in global mission, it is crucial for them to recognize this as apostolic-type ministry. Remember, apostolic ministry is released through apostolic structures.

The church faces three options: (1) develop a relationship with an existing mission organization through which the church can express its apostolic initiative, (2) develop a new organization to serve as the apostolic structure, or (3) some combination of these two.

Benefits of a church partnering with an existing mission organization:

- The organizational structure is already in place.
- The government already recognizes it as a charity.
- A process for receiving and managing funds is in place.
- There is expertise in travel arrangements, visa requirements, etc.
- There is experience in cross-cultural ministry.
- There is help connecting with others in the target area.

Areas to be addressed:

- Is there compatibility of ethos between church and organization?
- How will the two establish effective communication?
- How will decisions be made? By whom? Through what process?
- How will ownership of the church's vision be preserved?

• How will the leadership of the church and the organization interface?

Benefits of a church developing a new organization:

• The church may feel more authentic ownership of the mission.
• Businesspeople, lawyers, accountants, etc. will find a role.
• Issues of compatibility and ethos are easily addressed.
• This structure can start small and grow as needed.
• Communication between the church and the structure is simplified.
• The church will develop expertise in cross-cultural ministry.

Areas to be addressed:

• Developing a partnership with at least one mission organization.
• Being proactive in learning cross-cultural realities.
• Connecting effectively with other organizations and partnerships.
• Including people on the board with experience outside the church.
• Not sending workers to the target culture until the church is ready.
• Sustaining costly cross-cultural ministry long term.

Implications for Mission Organizations Today

How can people in mission organizations learn to work more effectively with local churches?

I went to India as a missionary when I was twenty-six years old. It soon became clear that, for the most part, the gospel would spread across India through my Indian brothers and sisters, not through me. If I were going to have a meaningful role, it would be because they invited me to have one with them.

What would free them to allow me to have such a role? In a word, attitude. I would have to be among them as a servant, to communicate a deep respect for them, their country, their culture, and their hopes and dreams. And to communicate that respect, I had to have that respect at the deepest levels of my being. It was far more than a communication issue. It was a heart issue.

I would have to lay aside all I had been socialized to believe and feel about being an American—the idea that "America is the greatest country in the world." If I believed that, it would come out. No. I was a citizen of heaven, called by Jesus to be his servant. That was so much higher. It was not that I had to be disrespectful to my country. Absolutely not. God decides our country of origin. And it was not that I did not have God-given gifts to offer the people of India. I did.

But in order to be able to share those things, the people of India had to extend the invitation to me. And in order for them to do that, they had to trust my heart. And in order for them to be able to trust my heart, they had to be able to see my heart, revealed in my actions as we shared life together.

> *The skills missionaries must learn to relate effectively to the culture they serve are the same skills needed to relate effectively to the local church.*

Trust has to be earned, and that takes time and investment. These things are well known among effective missionaries.

What Is the Process for Missionaries to Connect with the Local Church?

- We allow the Lord to cleanse us from all attitudes of superiority, the belief that we are the experts and the church is not.
- We biblically and authentically learn a high view of the church. We go as a learner with the attitude of a servant, humility, and respect.
- We recognize that the church has strengths we do not in the areas of spiritual gifting and life experience. These strengths are urgently required in the work of mission. (This does not reduce the strengths we have been given. As we honor the church, we free the church to honor us. This opens the way for mutual enrichment.)
- We must be free of all ulterior motives. We cannot use the church to advance our ministry or our organization. Self-serving motivation will show through. We go in the spirit of the kingdom of God.
- When we encounter areas in which the church is not yet mature, which we surely will, we learn to respond in a mature way. We become part of the solution.
- We grow to understand that being grafted into a local church will pay big dividends. If we will be serving cross-culturally for an extended time, we will need a spiritual, emotional, and financial support base:

  - This will take effort on our parts, especially in light of demanding travel schedules. It might slow us down, but it will make us much more effective. Is our goal to get to the field as quickly as possible or to be effective there for the long haul?
  - It will give us a first-hand understanding of local church life. How can one who has never been a vital part of a church be

effective in planting churches cross-culturally?

- Learning the ways of the local church is equally as important as learning the language and culture of our target people. We should be willing to invest as much time with it as we do preparing for the target people.
- Learning to submit to a local church is a process that forms the human sprit toward the likeness of Jesus.

Learning to relate to the local church in a godly way is not just a structure issue. It is a character issue.

Against all hope, Abraham in hope believed and so became the father of many nations. (Rom. 4:18)

God is calling us to believe him for the impossible. He is the Creator. He is omnipotent. Nothing is impossible for him. But the world is lost. The forces of hell are arrayed against God, against his Son, and against his Church. Entire nations are imprisoned behind walls of spiritual darkness. This is unacceptable. The Church must stand up and say no!

We look at ourselves. We look at our world through the perspectives and value systems that we have allowed our society to form in us. We look with human eyes and humanistic thinking. We limit reality to what seems rational. And we are afraid and cannot believe.

God is calling us, in every word of Scripture, to a radically different viewpoint. He is calling us to real reality, his reality. He is showing himself as the God of the impossible and the God of grace who works the impossible through the weak, the frail, and the vulnerable. He is calling us to a passion for the impossible.

CHAPTER 14

A Call to Faith

$\mathbf{G}$od is calling his Church to believe him for the impossible. God is calling us to trust him to work beyond the borders where human rationale would say we must stop. Look at what the Holy Spirit can cram into just five verses in Hebrews 11:8–12.

What Does It Look Like When God Calls His Servants?

God called Abraham. Biblical faith is always a response to God's initiative—a scriptural promise, a set of circumstances, or an inner sense of God's calling. It is not rooted in self-will. It is a response of humble obedience. Magic is man trying to manipulate the supernatural for his own selfish ends. Man is front and center. That is not faith.

Faith is God's design. It is his way of revealing himself and manifesting his power in the affairs of men. The human never gets the attention or receives the credit. The sense is always that "This is the hand of God." If the end result is that man is honored, it is not faith or God.

God has called his Church to the nations. All authority in heaven and earth has been given to Jesus. He has promised to be with us always. God has taken the initiative. He awaits our humble and obedient response.

God called Abraham to go. God calls us from a place that feels secure (although in our will, it is actually very insecure) to a place that feels insecure (although in God's will, it is totally secure).

God's call to India is still fresh in my memory. One particular chapel service stands out to me. I was in theological seminary. I was grappling with God's call. On the one hand, I loved my studies, my books, and the recognition I was getting as a good student. On the other hand, my heart was cold and empty, and I was experiencing a

> *God calls us from a place that feels secure to a place that feels insecure.*

deep hunger for more of God. And God was calling. In the chapel service, we sang a hymn that includes these lines:

We may trust Him fully all for us to do.
They who trust Him wholly find Him wholly true[8]

I was learning Greek, Hebrew, and theology. But I had never been in a place where all I had was God. I had never forsaken all. I was a Christian, but I had retained ultimate control of my affairs. I remember tears streaming down my face as I walked out of that service. I knew in my heart I had decided to trust him wholly.

I spent the next five years in India. They were years of uncertainty. It seemed there was never any money. I traveled more than half of the time, visiting itinerant evangelistic teams. I often slept on a train station platform or along the side the road. I could easily carry everything I owned with me.

These were some of the most wonderful, fruitful, fulfilling years of my life. God formed me in foundational ways. I learned tons more from my Indian brothers and sisters than they ever learned from me. And God gave me my wife. All I had was God, and I experienced firsthand that he is all I need.

God called Abraham to a place he would later receive. There almost always seems to be a time gap between when we respond in faith and when we receive that for which God called us to trust him. The gap is God's time for confirmation. It is one thing to trust God in a moment. It is quite another to live out that trust day after day, year after year. There were twenty-five years between the time God promised Abraham and Sarah a son and the birth of Isaac.

We say we trust him. How do we know? How deep does it go? "Remember how the LORD your God led you all the way in the desert these forty years, to humble you and to test you in order to know what was in your heart" (Deut. 8:2).

God called Abraham to a place he would later receive as his inheritance. What kind of inheritance has real, enduring value?

Today we live in the midst of great material wealth. We are regularly encouraged to plan for our retirement, to write our wills, and to form our trusts. It is a "wise" person who makes provision for his or her legacy to be passed along. Many are anticipating the day they will receive a material inheritance.

When God called me to lay aside further studies and go to India, I had an older man in my life who was a cherished friend. He was outwardly very successful. He saw real potential in

> *It is one thing to trust God in a moment. It is quite another to live out that trust day after day, year after year.*

me. He spoke of leaving me an inheritance. Then I made my decision to go to India. It made no sense to him. He thought that to leave my studies and abandon future success in order to go to India was the epitome of irresponsibility. We drifted apart.

He died some thirty years later. He died alone. He may have died from loneliness. He died surrounded by the fruits of selfishness. His will was a written record of the vindictiveness of his soul. Now, a short time later, it is as though the memory of his life has already been swept from the earth. Where is the meaningful legacy? Money and success could not establish it.

I remember when Mother Teresa of Calcutta died. She was a European Christian living in predominantly Hindu and Muslim India. She died in poverty. She held no claim to wealth, social standing, or power. But all India mourned her death and celebrated her life. Her legacy is written in the lives of millions. She received an inheritance from God through her simple obedience of faith that will endure for generations.

God is calling the Church to a lasting inheritance. It is an inheritance woven into human history because it is deposited into human lives. It is an inheritance established through the humble, obedient response to the call of God. It is an inheritance where people say, "I have received from God through him or her."

Unreached peoples are waiting for the next generation of Mother Teresas to bring them the gospel of the kingdom. When those who are called of God respond in humble obedience and faith, forsaking all to follow God's call, God will free them from the deception of reputation and riches and give them a precious and lasting inheritance, a "city with foundations, whose architect and builder is God" (Heb. 11:10).

By faith Abraham obeyed and went. Faith and obedience are two sides of the same coin, impossible to separate. Only the one who believes can obey; only the one who obeys can believe. Faith will be expressed by obedience or it will quickly wither. Obedience can only come from faith; otherwise, it will come from self-effort and will quickly exhaust its energy.

Giving only verbal assent to the call and commands of God is what Jesus called hypocrisy. It is like taking a part in a play and learning the lines of a character that is not us. That is okay for the theater. But when life becomes performing a role that is not who

> *Faith and obedience are two sides of the same coin, impossible to separate. Only the one who believes can obey; only the one who obeys can believe.*

we are on the inside, we become a shell. This is not the life to which God has called us. This is not Christianity.

Disobedience is death; it is like drinking poison. Obedience is life; it is the way of fullness and fulfillment. It was the way Abraham walked. Not perfectly. Abraham, although known as the father of all who live by faith, at times struggled and felt defeated (Rom. 4:11–12). But, in the end, he believed and obeyed. That is what God is calling us to do.

By faith Abraham, in God's way and time, was given descendants as numerous as the stars in the sky. "Abraham fell facedown; he laughed and said to himself, 'Will a son be born to a man a hundred years old? Will Sarah bear a child at the age of ninety?' And Abraham said to God, 'If only Ishmael might live under your blessing!'" (Gen. 17:17–18).

We are like Abraham. We father our Ishmaels and ask God to accept them in place of that for which he is calling us to trust him. Our Ishmaels represent our self-will, our impatience, our wish for control. We try to manipulate God and ask him to cooperate with us. He won't. He waits until we are ready to let go and trust him fully.

> *We father our Ishmaels and ask God to accept them in place of that for which he is calling us to trust him.*

After Abraham had gone through his struggles of faith, after he had doubted, after he had passed Sarah off as his sister, after he had fathered Ishmael out of unbelief and disobedience, and after twenty-five years, when he finally came to the point of rest and surrender, we read these words:

"Now the LORD was gracious to Sarah as he had said, and the LORD did for Sarah what he had promised. Sarah became pregnant and bore a son to Abraham in his old age, at the very time God had promised him" (Gen. 21:1–2).

God is waiting. He is waiting to pour forth his grace, his power, and his blessing. He is waiting to do the impossible among unreached peoples. He is ready to hear our prayers, send forth workers, break the power of darkness, and manifest his kingdom among men. He does not want to, and will not, do this without us.

"Against all hope, Abraham in hope believed and so became the father of many nations" (Rom. 4:18).

---

[8]Frances R. Havergal, "Like a River Glorious," first published in *Hymns of Consecration and Faith*, 1876. Public Domain. Music by James Mountain. Music copyright Marshal, Morgan and Scott.

So Peter was kept in prison, but the church was earnestly praying to God for him. (Acts 12:5)

Prayer is one of the most delightful, fulfilling, healing, and meaningful experiences available to human beings. It is two-way communication with God—our benefactor, Creator, and Father. It is the environment for which we were designed, as a fish is for water. It is an activity that can be easily learned from others and practiced with them. This is one reason why churches are such wonderful contexts for powerful, Spirit-energized prayer movements. People can pray together!

There is a sense in which being with God and learning his heart makes us rebellious. We learn that entire nations remain without the gospel, shaking their fists at God and his Church, and something within us rises up and says, "This must be changed!" That is visceral motivation for focused, extended, committed, corporate intercession. We join with our brothers and sisters in Christ to say, "O God, for your glory, tear down that spiritual wall!"

No pursuit of God's design for local churches in global mission would be adequate without a call to prayer. Prayer paves the way for kingdom advance like nothing else. And because the local church is local, its members have the chance to pray for extended periods together. There is power in individual prayer in the prayer closet. There is also awesome power in intercession with others in the congregation. Prayer, from genuinely humble hearts, bound in the unity of the Spirit, filled with faith and love, is the engine of kingdom advance.

CHAPTER 15

A Call to Corporate Prayer

N ations of the world that have been sealed in spiritual darkness for centuries are in that condition for a reason. They are not going to be penetrated for God's kingdom just because we are enthusiastic about doing so. They are held hostage by spiritual forces that can only be broken by the power of God. And there is the sense in which God waits to release his power in new dimensions until his people are ready. There is hardly a more genuine expression of the Church's desire for God's glory than for us to set aside extended periods for humble, believing, disciplined, God-honoring prayer.

This chapter is a call for us to carve out of our schedules extended periods for corporate prayer. I am well aware that we all feel there is no time to do this. But as we, motivated by faith and obedience, make the necessary choices in our days and weeks to allocate time to this, we find God arranges for the things we need to get done. And in the process, we are refreshed, renewed, taught, and empowered in the inner person. It takes time to know God, to hear his voice, and to

> *There is hardly a more genuine expression of the Church's desire for God's glory than for us to set aside extended periods for humble, believing, disciplined, God-honoring prayer.*

intercede for all nations, especially for the nation(s) our church is ministering among.

What Is the Basis of Our Call to Extended Periods of Prayer?

The example of men and women of God in the Old Testament. When Moses needed to receive instructions from God, he spent forty days and forty nights on Mt. Sinai (Deut. 9:9). When David's enemies pursued him, he repeatedly sought the presence of God. When Elijah was called to bring revival to Israel, he went alone to Mt. Carmel and heard God's still, small voice. It is difficult to point to a single man or woman of God in the Old Testament who was not a man or woman of extended periods of prayer.

The teaching of the Old Testament. "This is what the LORD says, he who made the earth, the LORD who formed it and established it...'Call to me and I will answer you and tell you great and unsearchable things you do not know'" (Jer. 33:2–3). We find a multitude of Old Testament passages on prayer. Men and women of God in the Old Testament taught what they lived.

The example of Jesus. Early in his ministry, Jesus arose early in order to give himself to prayer (Mark 1:35). The night before he named his disciples, he spent the whole night in prayer (Luke 6:12). When his death was hours away, he retreated to a quiet place to pray and urged his disciples to pray with him (Matt 26:36–46). Jesus was a man given to extended prayer.

The teaching of Jesus. Jesus taught often on prayer. "Ask [keep on asking] and it will be given to you; seek [keep on seeking] and you will find; knock [keep on

> *Jesus taught his disciples to pray by taking them with him into prayer. He taught what he lived.*

knocking] and the door will be opened to you" (Matt. 7:7). He taught his disciples to pray by taking them with him into prayer. He taught what he lived.

The example of the New Testament Church. One of the spontaneous activities of the new church formed at Pentecost was prayer (Acts 2:42). When the Church faced its earliest seasons of persecution, Acts tells us its instinctual response was extended corporate prayer (Acts 4:23, 12:5). As the Church grew, the apostles appointed deacons to take on more of the administrative load so they could give themselves to prayer (Acts 6:4). It was during an extended season in prayer that God spoke to the leaders of the church at Antioch and indicated the time had come for Saul and Barnabas to be set apart and sent among the Gentiles (Acts 13:1–3).

The teaching of the New Testament Church. The teaching of the New Testament Church emerged out of its life experience. It is rich in the subject of prayer: "And pray in the Spirit on all occasions with all kinds of prayer and requests" (Eph. 6:18).

The example of men and women of God in Church and mission history. Study the history of mission and the Church. Read the writings of the Church fathers, the great devotional classics, and diaries of kingdom pioneers. Wherever we look into our spiritual heritage, wherever there has been life and vitality, there has been an understanding of the delight and power of prayer. One example comes from the diary of Hudson Taylor, one of God's pioneers in China who had a profound influence on the modern missionary movement.

> *Wherever we look into our spiritual heritage, wherever there has been life and vitality, there has been an understanding of the delight and power of prayer.*

On Sunday, June 25, 1865, unable to bear the sight of a congregation of a thousand or more Christian people rejoicing in their own security, while millions were perishing for lack of knowledge, I wandered out on the sands alone, in great spiritual agony, and there the Lord conquered my unbelief, and I surrendered myself to God for this service...There and then I asked Him for twenty-four fellow-workers, two for each of eleven inland provinces which were without a missionary, and two for Mongolia; and in writing the petition on the margin of the Bible I had with me, I returned home with a heart enjoying rest such as it had been a stranger to for months...I had previously prayed, and asked prayer, that workers might be raised up for the eleven unoccupied provinces,...but had not surrendered myself to be their leader.[9]

The reality of spiritual warfare. Spiritual opposition to prayer often makes prayer extremely difficult. Regularly scheduled times of prayer with others can be enormously helpful in breaking through this opposition. There is power in united, believing prayer, which we do not experience alone. The more we work, and sense the futility of what we do from our own resources, the more convinced we become that prayer is the most rational activity we can engage in. Only God can penetrate the enemy's strongholds.

From the beginning of the ministry of the ship *Logos,* there was a certain country we especially wanted to visit. The country was very unreached, and many of us had been praying for years for God to work there. In this country, it was very difficult to share Christ, and we wondered how we would get a ship there that had one hundred and forty people from twenty different countries without attracting unwanted attention. Then, in the fifth year of *Logos'* ministry, our itinerary brought us into the region where this country is located.

On the ship, we had daily times of prayer, and, once a week, we had an extended half-night of prayer. For months, knowing that we would be in the vicinity, we prayed that God would open the door to visit. Prayer groups in many parts of the world joined in this prayer effort. And God opened the door! In a very specific answer to prayer, we received permission to visit for ten days! Significant restrictions were placed on what we could do, but we wanted to visit so badly we were prepared to live with just about anything.

The morning we were coming into the harbor, the pilot bringing *Logos* into the berth collided with a local ferry. By the time we reached the berth, *Logos* was impounded and unable to leave the country. We had prayed for so long that we would be able to visit, and now, all of a sudden, we were unable to leave! Boy, did God know what he was doing or what?

He gave us a month there. Quietly, through simple, transparent, love-based friendships, local people came to learn of the faith in Jesus shared by all of the ship's company. I still remember the final Sunday. As the ship crew and staff gathered in the dining room for worship, local people who had made their way in found themselves in the presence of Jesus as he inhabited the praises of his people. God had performed a miracle. He had taken a ship and over one hundred followers of Jesus into a very unreached place, manifested his glory, and brought individuals to faith. The key was not the ship or an international community. They were the instruments. The key was prayer—extended, compassionate, faith-filled prayer—and a God full of mercy and compassion, waiting to respond to the sincere prayers of his Church.

Keeping us from seeking glory for ourselves. When a church becomes serious about prayer, it is a statement of humility and dependence. The fellowship is saying, "This is not our work but God's. We are relying on him alone." This attitude sets the stage for God to work. When the answers come, it is clear that this is the hand of God. These works of God release worship, thanksgiving, and joy. Those who see what has really taken place spiritually reject any praise that comes to them. Glory belongs to God alone.

Months before God gave us the second of the Operation Mobilization ships, the *Doulos*, we knew in our spirits that she would be coming. There had been four years of intensive, focused prayer by so many. God had already provided much of the needed crew and staff. We started taking steps to move experienced crew members ashore to pray for the ship so that newer arrivals could gain experience on *Logos*. But we still lacked two crucial components: the actual ship that would become the *Doulos* and much of the money needed to buy her. And we could do little about either.

Then God showed us the ship. It was the *Franca C.*, owned by an Italian firm headquartered in Genoa. It met our specifications. I still remember when we saw her for the first time. She was pulling into Venice for a brief stop on a Saturday morning in August. We went on board, were given a thorough tour, and ended our time by praying together at the forward end of the main lounge. I think we all shared an overwhelming feeling that this was God's ship. I know I did.

We still did not have all the money, but by faith our board made the decision to move forward with the purchase. As the time for closing the sale approached, we watched money come into our bank account from all over—Germany, Switzerland, Sweden, Singapore, the United Kingdom, Holland, the United States, and other countries. It all had to be converted into U.S. dollars. Would there be enough?

On the morning of the closing, we met with the owners. After all transfers were tallied, we were $400 short! Several of us stood around the table and reached into our pockets for our wallets. I remember taking out the money I had for the return train fare to Germany and placing it on the table with other cash people had. When we walked out of that office, all we had was documentation that our company owned the *Franca C.* That was twenty-five years ago. Since then, many millions of people have been touched through the ministry of the ship in hundreds of ports. It all happened, not through clever people or sophisticated strategies, but because there is a God of grace and mercy who moves mountains when ordinary, frail people pray.

Hearing God and sensing his heart together. Both individuals and churches need to hear God, to feel his heart, and to receive his direction. Why don't we hear God more often? Is he not speaking? Sometimes we need to mature in our ability to listen. Listening takes time. We must learn how to do it, and we learn by practicing. There are inner barriers that need to be removed. When a group hears God together, the result is a shared experience that produces focused, unified action.

> When a group hears God together, the result is a shared experience that produces focused, unified action.

I am thinking of a church that was preparing to send a church planting team to an unreached people group. In this case, the team was to be led by their senior pastor! God had used him to start the church and to establish the members in the faith. Now it was God's time for him to be sent out to do it again.

The church had been in prayer over this for many months. What unreached people group was God leading to? Who should go? What should be the strategy? How should the work be funded? Prayer extended down to more specific practical needs like the provision of the initial housing the team would need. The people of the church really owned this.

I was in the church service one Sunday morning when the senior pastor reported to the congregation about his recent visit to the target city. It was nearly time for the team to leave, and he had gone to find accommodations for them. He had only been able to have a week there. After a couple of days, things looked really hopeless. Then, through a very unlikely series of events, the perfect place opened up. The team had the accommodations they needed not only to go but also to begin the work of church planting.

The church was ecstatic. There was such a feeling of worship for what God had done. The sense in this congregation was that God had heard their prayers. The provision of the accommodation was not only an answer to the prayers of the team but also to the prayers of the church. Prayer had played a powerful role in giving the whole church ownership of the mission.

Responding to all there is to pray about. In the busyness of life and ministry, many issues come at us for decision and action at a moment when there is little time to pray. Regular, scheduled sessions of group prayer provide the opportunity to saturate past actions, present dilemmas, and pending decisions with prayer. There is awesome protection in entering into a season of activity that has been saturated with believing prayer.

Getting in tune with God. Am I in touch with the condition of my heart? What things lurk there that the Holy Spirit wants to make me aware of? When do I bring these things to God for his cleansing and renewal? What is the condition of my relationship with my brother or sister? Is there corrective action I need to take? How is God leading me? Our church? Our team? What does God want to say to me, to us? Extended times in God's presence serve as planned opportunities to allow such interaction with God to take place.

Practical Helps for Corporate Prayer

Here are some practical keys for leading extended times of group prayer:

Balance intercession with worship. Intercession is work; it depletes us. Worship is refreshing and renewing; it restores us. God is raising up and anointing leaders of worship. Find them and incorporate them into extended prayer times.

Balance time spent giving requests with time spent in prayer. The danger is for talk and prayer requests to dominate. When this happens, the effectiveness of prayer times erodes. There is almost nothing the enemy hates more than prayer. If he can't keep us from the prayer meeting, he will try to keep us from praying there. Satan will contest a commitment to prayer. Talking with each other is not why we have come together. It doesn't accomplish God's work. Talking with Jesus does.

> *There is almost nothing the enemy hates more than prayer. If he can't keep us from the prayer meeting, he will try to keep us from praying there.*

Vary the size of the group(s). Depending on the size of the total group, pray at times all together, at times in larger groups, at times in smaller groups, at times two by two, and at times as individuals. Sameness kills.

Ask people to pray short prayers in a loud voice. Sometimes it is helpful to get people to stand. God does not have a short attention span, but some of our fellow prayers will. And God is not hard of hearing, but if the group is large, and if someone prays in a soft voice with his head buried in his hands, others will not be able to join with him in prayer. It can be embarrassing when someone starts to pray while someone else is already praying.

Encourage freedom in body positions. Kneeling is very biblical, but it can become tiring after a while. We can also grow weary while sitting, but standing wakes us up. To pray while walking can be very good; encourage people to keep their eyes open! Freedom to vary body positions helps to establish an atmosphere of informality and freedom. Encourage people to take their shoes off if they desire.

Have written-out, short prayer requests. Printed pages with requests can achieve this, or requests can be projected onto the wall. When there are a lot of requests, smaller groups can each focus on a different set of requests so the group as a whole can cover more territory.

Consider a short fruit break. This is especially helpful for extended prayer times late in the evening or through the night. A basket of apples can provide a real boost. There could be some for whom water, fruit juices, or even coffee might be helpful.

Encourage people to share Bible verses. This can be done during another short break from prayer. You can suggest a theme, like prayer, faith, or verses that God has recently used to speak to people. Encourage people to share any impressions or pictures they see as the prayer time goes on.

"If you remain in me and my words remain in you, ask whatever you wish, and it will be given you. This is to my Father's glory, that you bear much fruit" (John 15:7–8).

---

[9]Ralph D. Winter and Steven C. Hawthorne, eds., *Perspectives on the World Christian Movement* (Pasadena, Calif.: William Carey Library,

**I shall . . . devote myself to . . . that congregation
whose servant I became. . . . Under her protection,
enjoying her care, and influenced by her spirit,
I shall go to distant nations who are ignorant of Jesus.**
—Nicolaus Ludwig von Zinzendorf[10]

*We have so far considered a number of different
themes—God's heart for all nations, the potential within
each individual, the power of Christian community, the
magnificence of the local church, and the indispensable role
of apostolic ministry. We have taken a close look at faith
and prayer. Let's now treat ourselves to a delightful account
of one Christian community whose story integrates all these
into a seamless and inspiring whole.*

*Our English-speaking accounts of mission history
may not inform us about the Moravians, a group whose
roots go back to present-day Germany and the Czech
Republic. But a brief overview of their experience offers us
a rich perspective on how the gospel can be transplanted
into other cultures from a local church. The Moravians are a
heart-warming example of what this book is all about.*

> *The Moravians were the first Protestants to
> put into practice the idea that the evangeli-
> zation of the heathen is the duty of the
> church as such. Hitherto it had been a part
> of colonial policy, or had been espoused by
> missionary societies. It was this concept,
> carried out at the cost of blood, sweat, and
> tears, that made the Moravian mission so
> influential. No church better illustrates the
> total apostolate. —William J. Danker[11]*

*Beginning in 1722, a church of six hundred people
matured into the most significant Protestant missionary
movement of the eighteenth century. How did they do it?
What were the keys?*

CHAPTER 16
The Moravians

In 1722 a group of Moravian families began to emigrate out of their homeland in what is now the Czech Republic and settle on the estate of Count Nicolaus Ludwig von Zinzendorf in the German province of Saxony. These Moravians were spiritual descendants of the persecuted followers of John Hus, who had been burned at the stake for his faith in Prague in 1415. They belonged to a Protestant tradition that pre-dated Luther.

Zinzendorf, a member of Europe's high aristocracy, was born in 1700. He was a member of the court of his native Saxony and a cousin by marriage to the king of Denmark. At the age of ten, he was enrolled in the Paedagogium at Halle and came under the influence of August Hermann Francke and the Pietists, a holiness movement among German Protestants.

The East India mission had been started only four years earlier, and Zinzendorf heard reports of what God was doing beyond Europe. He even met some of the missionaries involved. Francke oversaw many charitable institutions and business enterprises and funded outreach through donations and business ventures.

Seeking a place in which to freely live out their life in Christ, the Moravians established a village called Herrnhut, meaning "(under) the Lord's watch," on land given to them by Zinzendorf. There they built their homes and common buildings, such as a church, a home for widows, places of business, etc. The community grew.

In 1731 Zinzendorf attended the coronation of King Christian VI of Denmark. There he met people from outside Europe who had never heard the name of Christ. Gripped with a sense of urgency to respond to this situation, he returned to Herrnhut and shared with the church what had been impressed upon him. Together they sought the Lord. Within a year, two craftsmen from their group volunteered to take the gospel to peoples in the West Indies.

In 1732 the Moravians sent their first missionary team to St. Thomas in the Caribbean. In the next twenty years, teams were sent to Greenland (1733), North America's Indian territories (1734), Surinam (1735), South Africa (1736), the Samoyedic peoples of the Artic (1737), Algiers and Sri Lanka 1740), China (1742), Persia (1747), and Abyssinia and Labrador (1752).[12]

By the end of the first decade of these mission initiatives, seventy cross-cultural witnesses had been sent from a church of six hundred. Fifty years later, a total of three hundred had been sent out, more than all Protestants before them put together.[13]

> By the end of the first decade of the Moravian mission initiatives, seventy cross-cultural witnesses had been sent from a church of six hundred.

Awesome! What enabled them do it?

Components of the Moravians' Success

They shared a heritage of sacrifice. The Moravians' forefathers had been persecuted for their faith. Suffering was not strange or abnormal to them. Such experiences of God and his ways prepared them to follow the crucified Jesus unconditionally and to embrace the personal costs inherent in bringing him to the nations. God had sovereignly prepared them for kingdom fruitfulness.

Much of the Church today is formed by a culture of permissiveness. Any suggestion that restricts us from indulging whatever appetite we choose, whenever we choose, fills many with outrage. We are often blind to the destruction such conditioning brings to human lives, ours and others'.

Such values have pervasively formed Christ's Church. They make Jesus' call to follow him in the shadow of his cross sound unattractive, out of date, and irrelevant. They erode our capacity to respond to our Master's "all nations" mandate. Suffering is a normal part of life when we become a disciple of Jesus. He teaches us that following him involves leaving our nets and taking up our cross.

> *Suffering is a normal part of life when we become a disciple of Jesus. He teaches us that following him involves leaving our nets and taking up our cross.*

Along with suffering, he teaches us about life, joy, love, and intimacy with God. When we suffer for him, we look back and think, "Whatever I have given up was nothing compared to what I have found in him." God is serious about the gospel being taken to every nation. To do it, he will raise up a people prepared to sacrifice.

They shared a heritage of celebration. For the Moravians, suffering produced not bitterness and self-pity but joy, thankfulness, and worship. The Lamb was worthy, and they needed to say so. They had already published the first Protestant hymnal in 1501, years before Martin Luther tacked his Ninety-five Theses on the castle church door at Wittenberg, and since then had produced a large collection of worship music. It is reported that during the commissioning service of the first missionary team, they sang one hundred hymns. Worship empowered everything they did—their prayers, their faith, their sacrifice, and their shared life.

As apostolic-type teams were sent forth from Herrnhut in

increasing numbers, their global influence grew. One of the most fascinating examples of this was the impact they had on John Wesley, which led him to find a personal faith in Christ. Wesley visited Herrnhut, and the following entry from his journal gives a firsthand account of the atmosphere he found there:

> Today was the Intercession-day, when many strangers were present, some of whom came twenty or thirty miles. I would gladly have spent my life here; but my Master, calling me to labor in another part of his vineyard, on Monday, August 14, 1738, I was constrained to take my leave of this happy place...O when shall this Christianity cover the earth as the "waters cover the sea?"[14]

They were gripped by an inner imperative that Christ be made known among all peoples on earth. Their motivation for mission was not compulsion or guilt but worship and joy. Jesus was worthy. It was inherently obvious that all nations must hear of him and be given every opportunity to come to know, to love, to obey, and to worship him.

As reports came back from the first teams and as the church realized doors were opening to the gospel, energy for what God was doing spread throughout the community. Their worship fueled their conviction that Christ could only be appropriately honored by receiving praise from every nation. Their twenty-four-hour prayer ministry deepened their sense of participating in that a reality.

This passion rested not just with those with a special interest in missions but flourished throughout the fellowship. It was central to the experience of every person.

They viewed God's global mission as the responsibility of the whole church. The whole church had received forgiveness and grace. The whole church loved the Savior. The whole church needed a God-sized purpose beyond themselves in which they could invest themselves. Why then shouldn't the whole church embrace the privilege of making him known among all nations? This understanding found expression in every aspect of life—in their worship, their prayer meetings, their family traditions, and their work.

> *The Moravians' worship fueled their conviction that Christ could only be appropriately honored by receiving praise from every nation.*

The more family members were sent forth, the more the rest of the church felt ownership and responsibility to support the group's efforts. Herrnhut had developed an interdependent economy and social services structure, and those remaining behind had to step into responsibilities vacated by those going out. A wonderful example of this is how business enterprises became engines to fuel the missionary outreach.

They did things together. The Moravians had built Herrnhut together. They pursued their daily work together. If the community needed a certain trade, someone would take on this responsibility for the sake of the group. They worshipped together, prayed together, worked interdependently, and made decisions together.

So when they began to send out cross-cultural witnesses, it was natural for them to approach this together. The whole community joined ranks to make it possible to send out more. And when witnesses were sent out, they were sent in teams. These Moravians understood the power of groups.

They made no distinctions between clergy and laity. The Moravians understood that every believer had a vocational calling from God and was to serve him and others in that vocation. No calling was superior in God's eyes over any other, whether one served in Herrnhut or as a cross-cultural witness. Everyone, not just a select few, was seen as a participant, a contributor. There were no spectators.

The Moravians were a lay movement. When apostolic teams

were sent out, it was anticipated that members would continue to work in their trades. As the mission movement grew, more and more business people were sent along with those who focused on evangelism. These would start businesses to fund themselves and their other teammates.

> *The Moravians were a lay movement. When apostolic teams were sent out, it was fully anticipated that members would continue to work in their trades.*

Business people developed enterprises to facilitate the sending of more cross-cultural teams. This may have been one of the most significant contributions made by the Moravians to the worldwide cause of Christ. In our English-speaking tradition of missions, we are familiar with the role of the missionary doctor or teacher. But the concept of the missionary businessman is foreign to us. It is not part of our tradition. Why?

Business activities were developed at Herrnhut to help fund mission activities. However committed to giving and sacrificial living they may be, there is a limit to what six hundred people can fund from their own resources. An expanding outreach requires an expanding resource base.

One example of this was Abraham Dürninger, a businessman who came to Herrnhut seeking a spiritual home. In 1747 Zinzendorf asked him to take over the community's general store that was losing money. Over the next twenty-five years, Dürninger turned the store into a profit-making enterprise. He further developed an international business complex that was engaged in manufacturing as well as wholesale and retail commerce. Especially profitable was an international linen trade. From his profits, Dürninger turned over to church leadership large sums of money for further outreach. International trade was funding international mission. Dürninger's store is still in business in Herrnhut today!

They were committed to prayer. At Herrnhut, it was the practice to begin the day with group prayer. On weekends, the church would gather to hear reports from teams and intercede on their behalf. As early as 1727, a round-the-clock prayer watch began that continued for one hundred years. They were sending members of their own community, brothers and sisters who were precious to them, into some of the darkest places on earth. The enemy was not sitting still and accepting all this without challenging them on every turn. What a powerful component this commitment to prayer must have been to their overall mission success.

> *What if a movement of reproducing churches like the eighteenth century Moravians were catalyzed today?*

The principles by which the Moravians lived and ministered are principles God intends to be a normal part of every church. That the Moravian experience is so unusual and inspirational to us is tragic. Why are these principles and practices not widely known and experienced among us?

---

[10] William J. Danker, *Profit for the Lord: Economic Activities in Moravian Missions and the Basel Mission Trading Company* (Grand Rapids: Eerdmans, 1971) p. 16.

[11] W. Carey Moore, ed., "Christian History," *Christian History Magazine* 1, no. 1 (1982): 35.

[12] Winter and Hawthorne, eds., *Perspectives,* p. 206.

[13] W. Carey Moore, ed., "Christian History," p. 18.

[14] W. Carey Moore, ed., "Christian History," p. 30.

We missionaries have bought the problem. But we lack the resources required to solve the problem. —President of a mission organization

After twenty years as a missionary, much of which was spent as a senior leader of a large mission organization, I was looking for answers. Our organization faced awesome open doors for the gospel. Yet it seemed that, in whatever direction we turned, there was a corresponding dearth of resources. We needed more workers, more expertise, more prayer, more finances, and more pastoral ministry. We needed more of everything!

God gave me a day with a colleague who was the president of another highly respected large mission organization. I knew our organization's experience was not unique—every mission agency faced the same reality. As we sought answers together, he said to me, "You know, George, world evangelization is a problem, and we missionaries have bought the problem. But we lack the resources required to solve the problem."

"Our mistake," he continued, "is that world evangelization is not our problem alone. It is the responsibility of the whole Church. And God has placed a huge proportion of the resources required to solve this problem in local churches."

CHAPTER 17

Ownership

In this chapter, I want to place before you six theses. If we can agree on these, the ways in which we think about and approach missions will be fundamentally altered.

Six Theses of Ownership in Mission

1. Starting churches among unreached peoples is the highest priority for completing Christ's Great Commission. Now the minute I say that, I know some will hear me say, "Every Christian should be planting churches among unreached peoples, and anybody who is not doing that is a second-class Christian." I want to clarify: I do not mean that. I do not believe that.

I want to validate, in the strongest possible terms, the ministry passion that lies within each individual believer. Is it for the poor? Christian counseling? Youth ministry? Strengthening Christian families? Providing for Christian education? Ministries of healing? Something else? God has called his people to a range of ministries far wider than planting churches among unreached peoples. If you have had a long-lasting ministry passion in some specific area, the chances are very good that God has placed this desire within you. It needs to be affirmed, honored, developed, and released. Think with me for a moment not about *importance* but about *priority*.

Bill is a friend who has a passion to minister among the poor and underprivileged. His energy and compassion to do this are almost tangible. And God is bringing wonderful fruit through his life as he does it. Ministering among the poor and underprivileged is on the heart of God. He wants it to happen.

Bill's ministry is taking place in his home city. It is taking place because Bill is there, and Bill is there because the Church is there. Those who were responsible for bringing him to faith and nurturing his maturity are inseparable from the ministry he is carrying out. His ministry today is an extension of their ministry in the past.

It would be a mistake for Bill to leave what he is doing, at least right now, and go to plant churches among an unreached people group. God has not called him to do that. He has called him to the poor and underprivileged in his home city. But, and here is the crucial point, God also has a heart for the poor and underprivileged among unreached peoples. And virtually no ongoing ministry is taking place among them, because the Church is not there.

Therefore, our highest priority is to jump start the process of starting new churches among unreached peoples. Only in this way can ministry among the poor and underprivileged, and all the other ministries on God's heart, take place.

The good news is that we are not confronted here with an either/or choice. No. The capacity of Christ's Church is decidedly both/and. Bill doesn't have to stop what he is doing in his own city so that churches can be started among unreached cultures. There is no need to think of closing down the church and sending everybody halfway around the world. Such an idea is, of course, silly. It would be a disaster. It is not God's way. Less than one percent of all believers worldwide will have to leave home and go to an unreached people group for us to complete world evangelization.

Hear me. The best numbers I can find suggest that, at the time of this writing, there are approximately 6,600 unreached people groups in the world. And, *for every one unreached people group, there are some 600 local churches!* Stop for a minute and soak it in. We have, overwhelmingly, everything we could ever need to complete this task tomorrow (almost)!

Why have we not done it? What is wrong?

2. *Most Christians assume that the responsibility to start churches among unreached peoples lies with missionaries.* This is inherent in the way we have come to think about and approach missions. We have made missions a spectator sport. Most of us are sitting in the stands watching the players (missionaries) do their thing down on the field.

> *We have made missions a spectator sport. Most of us are sitting in the stands watching the players (missionaries) do their thing down on the field.*

I have just come from speaking at the Sunday services of a wonderful church that is beautifully and faithfully committed to missions. They are everything you would want to see in a missions-minded church. The ways in which they do missions are familiar.

The church:

- supports dozens of missionaries financially.
- has a big map in the church with a light on it for each missionary.
- has a framed picture of each missionary in the foyer.
- has visiting missionaries give reports during Sunday services.
- has events to help the whole church get to know the missionaries.

Now, I ask you, who are the players in the game, and who are the spectators?

One approach to rectify this condition and get everybody in the game is to give a sermon on the subject during the annual missions emphasis season. Challenge the people to get in the game!

How are they supposed to do this? Pray? Give money? Attend missions functions in the church? Anything more than that is something each person must figure out for himself or herself. When we challenge them to get in the game, there are no meaningful avenues available by which they can respond.

Sadly there is little in this approach that is vital, fulfilling, or meaningful to most people. The vast majority just can't relate. This approach easily triggers feelings of "ought" and "should." It does not connect people with vision, tap into spiritual gifting, invite personal expression, or fuel individual creativity and vitality. Mission feels, dare we be honest? irrelevant.

I recently heard a management saying that certainly rings true here: "Your system is perfectly designed to produce the results you are getting." If we want to change missions from a spectator sport where most Christians sit passively in the stands and watch the missionaries play the game, we must fundamentally redesign how we think about and approach missions.

The solution requires more than missionary conference pep rallies designed to impart missions enthusiasm, although

> *To change missions from a spectator sport where most sit in the stands watching the missionaries play the game, we must fundamentally redesign how we think about missions.*

more godly enthusiasm is certainly called for. Nor is the answer merely more information, although more of the right kind of information is crucial. No, there is the need for a whole new approach, a new way of structuring things, a new paradigm. Mission participation must be made meaningful. Rather than trying to discover better ways to cut down the tree we are currently sawing on, we need to realize that "Oops, it's the wrong tree!"

3. Missionaries lack the resources this task requires. We need more workers. We need more diversity in the spiritual gifts and callings of those who are going. In addition to evangelists and teachers, every ministry in the body of Christ is needed. We need a more vocationally diverse mission force. Effective entry and engagement with the culture among unreached peoples is often problematic for professional missionaries. It is usually much more accessible to business people, professionals, engineers, social workers, students, and so on.

We need more authority in spiritual warfare. Groups of worshippers and intercessors play a critical role in building the needed momentum. More familiar forms of witnessing must be accompanied by fighting against entrenched spiritual strongholds. We have a need for more money and more apostolic givers. Expanding Christ's kingdom among all nations needs more of everything. It is worthy of nothing less. Jesus is worthy of nothing less.

4. We Christians are investing a tiny percentage of our resources in completing this task; we don't sense ownership. I want to use the word *tokenism.* I do not intend to be unkind or harsh, but it is crucial that we think about obeying the last recorded words of our Lord ("make disciples of *all* nations") accurately and precisely.

We are dropping pennies into the plate. We are offering the Lord that which costs us virtually nothing. Let's look at two areas to help give meaning to this: numbers of workers and levels of giving.

Numbers of workers: At this writing, our best research shows there are about 400 million believers in the world. Of those, 200,000 are cross-cultural witnesses. That is 0.05 percent of us!

What will it take to finish the job? We have 6,600 unreached people groups. What if we could put one hundred new church planters in each one? To do so would bring the total number of cross-cultural witnesses to a little more than 0.2 percent of all believers on earth—hardly an over-reaction! And we would only need to send out something like one worker from every six churches. We can do this! Let's make this our goal and see how

> *What will it take to finish the job? To put one hundred new church planters in each remaining unreached people group, we would only need to send out one church planter from every six churches. Let's make this our goal and see how far it gets us!*

far it gets us! We don't need every believer to be a missionary, not by a long shot!

Levels of giving: When it comes to the giving patterns of God's people, the best figures I can find suggest:

- Christians give 2 percent of their income to Christian causes, including their local church, other Christian organizations in their social context, and foreign missions.
- Roughly 10 percent of this 2 percent (0.2 percent of Christians' income) is given to foreign missions. This includes work in officially designated reached people groups, where there are already significant numbers of local churches or missionaries. This is not to say that kingdom work in these areas is not legitimate. It certainly is. Again, we are not talking here about an either/or condition that requires us to choose one above the other.
- Christians give roughly 10 percent of this 0.2 percent (0.02 percent of their income) to church planting among unreached peoples. This means that, from every $100 we earn, we give 2 cents to starting churches among unreached peoples—the highest priority, but not necessarily the most important, the Church has to undertake.

Think for a minute of your own context—your church, your Christian friends, your personal giving priorities, and your decisions. Is what I have reported in this unscientific survey way out of line or more or less accurate? If completing Jesus' instructions to disciple every people is delayed, it is not because the financial resources are unavailable.

5. Perceptions must be reversed, and the ownership of global mission must be understood to belong to the whole Church. What might that look like? Picture your church fellowship arriving for services on Sunday morning only to discover that your building or meeting place had burned to the ground during the previous night. What might the response be?

- There might be a new sense of group. The emergency might bring people together. It might catalyze a deepened sense of shared experience, of bonding.
- There might be a new sense of ownership. "We must all do something about this," might be the prevailing feeling. This is our church, our crisis, and our responsibility. Nobody else is going to take ownership of this, so we must!
- People might revise their schedules. They might make time to pitch in and help. Some of these decisions might seem costly at first, but, in the end, people might discover deep personal enrichment in having made them.
- People not normally very active in church life might step forward, bringing with them skills in planning, building, funding, managing, or helping. They might discover that the opportunity to play a meaningful part is very fulfilling.
- People might revise their budgets. Sacrificial giving might suddenly seem reasonable in light of the new sense of emergency. In the end, people might discover they really did not have to sacrifice all that much since everybody chipped in.

Five years later, people might look back on the crisis as one of the best times the church has had together. Why would all this happen? There would be an experience of group ownership!

What might be the situation among your church fellowship if

my church's building burned down over a Saturday night? I could imagine your church being concerned and sympathetic. You might pray for us or even take an offering to help financially. Some members of your congregation might donate free time and expertise to help us rebuild. But you could not invest in what our church would be going through the way you could in your own reality. There simply would not be the same level of ownership.

Here is a critical factor in human motivation: People are more able to invest themselves in what they personally own than in what someone else owns.

What is the greater crisis: a church fellowship loosing its building or 6,600 unreached people groups who are without access to the gospel of Jesus Christ?

> *Here is a critical factor in human motivation: People are more able to invest themselves in what they personally own than in what someone else owns.*

6. *We should not hear the call of God's mission as another "ought" or "should" but as a grace-filled opportunity that offers natural, meaningful, fulfilling participation to every believer.* What might that look like?

- We might give a specifically defined piece of the remaining task (starting a church movement within each of the 6,600 remaining unreached people groups) to a local church.
- We might say to the church, "Complete this piece of the remaining task, using members of your church fellowship, according to the way God has called and gifted each person."
- We might further say to the church, "We will come alongside you to serve you, encourage you, and coach you in completing a piece of the remaining task for which

you have taken ownership."
- As the church successfully completes its piece of the remaining task, we can look for it to grow in its potential to undertake larger and larger pieces.

The following thoughts are offered somewhat tongue in cheek. But remember, we are talking about the need for a foundational change in how we think—a new structure, a new paradigm. In order to disrupt long-held behavior patterns and establish a new approach, we need to be ready to think in some radically new ways.

What would happen if we were to go back to the missions-minded church, in whose Sunday morning services I spoke recently, and make the following suggestions?

- In your approach to missions, shift from a response mode to a proactive mode. Do not ask, "Which missionaries do we want to support?" but rather, "What is the mission or task in which God is leading us to take ownership?"
- Study the situation in the world. Define the task remaining in your own words. This may sound daunting, but it really is not. You have wonderfully competent, godly people in your fellowship who can get their minds and hearts around this. What unreached people group(s) is God calling you to target? In what ways? Why are those ways strategic?
- Move the pictures of the missionaries ("cross-cultural witnesses" might be a better designation) on the wall in the foyer to a wall that is large enough for individual pictures of every person in the fellowship.
- Under the name of each missionary, write a ministry designation such as "cross-cultural witness," "teacher," "administrator," or whatever ministry the Lord has given them.

- Then take a picture of every person in the fellowship who is committed to praying for the completion of God's purpose among all peoples. Put their pictures on the wall among the cross-cultural witnesses. Write under each name "intercessor."
- Take a picture of every person who supports God's global purpose among all peoples administratively. Put their pictures up among the cross-cultural witnesses, the intercessors, and the donors. Write under each name "administrator."
- Take a picture of every person who gives pastoral care to those involved in God's global purpose. Put their pictures up among the cross-cultural witnesses, the intercessors, the donors, and the administrators. Write under each of their names "pastoral care."

You get the point. What other roles are people in your church playing? Giving hospitality? Serving in practical ways? Taking care of children? Take their pictures. Put them up on the wall. Write under their name what ministry they carry in God's global cause. They are players in the game too.

The end goal is for every person in the fellowship to have their picture on the wall of God's global mission. Now mission has ceased to be a spectator sport among you. Every person has moved from the stands onto the bench and into the game.

A feeling grows, expands, and becomes pervasive through the church. Mission is not something somebody else does who is far away and whom we hardly know. Mission is something we do—we all do—together.

That's ownership. And watch out, you are

> *Mission is not something somebody else does who is far away and whom we hardly know. Mission is something we do—we all do—together.*

creating something that looks like a modern Herrnhut! No telling what God will do with it.

So after I have completed this task, . . . I will go to Spain. (Rom. 15:28)

I can still see her in my mind—a short, middle-aged woman with a wholesomely appealing face and bearing. I immediately sensed she knew and loved my Lord and desired to honor him in every way she could. I had just finished speaking at her church, and, at least for that day, I stood in the place of "missions expert" in her mind.

As she began to speak with me, I learned that she was the chairperson of her church's missions committee and was concerned that the church was not connecting meaningfully with their missionaries. They financially supported sixty-four.

Then she asked me the question that was obviously most concerning her. "How can our church establish beneficial relationships with all our missionaries if we only see them one weekend every four years?" She stood by with pencil and paper in hand, waiting for the pearls of wisdom I would share with her.

Her genuineness freed me to speak the truth: "You can't."

CHAPTER 18

Strategic Focus

M̲ost churches cannot relate meaningfully with sixty-four missionaries. That doesn't reflect a lack in the churches so much as it highlights the need to reengineer the way in which we are doing missions.

Sometime back, many churches were thinking, "The more missionaries we can support, and the more countries they work in, the better our missions program will be." This was a period in which world maps appeared in church foyers with a pin in them for each missionary the church supported financially. In some circles, the goal was to have as many pins in the map as possible. More must be better!

Generally speaking, the motivation in this was commendable. Churches wanted to take the Great Commission seriously and to expand their involvement. Wonderful. Unfortunately the effects of approaching it this way were, over time, counterproductive both for the church and for the missionaries.

For missionaries, this approach reduced opportunities to communicate with the congregation about the work they were doing. Platform time had to be shared with a growing number of other missionaries. It also decreased levels of pastoral care for each missionary and lowered amounts of financial support. The church's resources had to be shared with more and more missionaries and mission projects.

I remember one missionary family who wanted to meet with

me about some of the challenges they were facing. During their furlough months they, with their children, drove from Maine to southern California. When they were initially raising their financial support, they found that many donors, both churches and individuals, thought in terms of giving relatively small monthly amounts to each missionary—ten, twenty-five, or fifty dollars. In order to raise the amount of support a family needs, how many giving units does this require? They had to keep adding supporting churches and individuals to reach their goal. Then, during furlough time, they felt obligated to visit them all and build relationships, although in most cases they could only give one weekend every four years or so.

For churches, the result of this thinking, in many cases, has been that missions has become depersonalized, perplexing, and largely irrelevant to the majority of people in the fellowship. It is not that they are unconcerned that the nations hear of Jesus; they just do not have the mental space to keep up with the number of missionaries, countries, and outreaches going on.

> *Most Christians are not unconcerned that the nations hear of Jesus; they just do not have the mental space to keep up with the number of missionaries, countries, and outreaches going on.*

What Is a Focused Approach to Missions?

A focused approach to missions

- is centered rather than diffused.
- is concentrated rather than diluted.
- resembles a rifle shot rather than a shotgun spray.
- is proactive rather than reactive.
- is objective and intentional rather than subjective and

without direction.

- is centered in mission rather than missionaries.
- moves from asking, "What missionaries are we going to support?" to asking, "What mission has God called us to undertake together, and what role does that play in completing God's all-peoples mission?"

As we unwrap this concept, we will see how both the church and the missionaries will benefit wonderfully.

In a church, here is what this might look like:

- In a context of seeking God for direction, the church chooses one unreached people group, rather than twenty to thirty countries or missionaries, with which to become involved.
- A strategy is developed in which the church asks, "How can we as a fellowship participate in seeing churches started among this people?"
- The church's prayer energy is centered on, although not limited to, the chosen people group. After all, the motivation for choosing one people group is that *all* peoples will be blessed.
- The church's mission education focuses on deepening the fellowship's understanding of conditions among the selected unreached people group.
- Short-term teams from the church concentrate on serving among this unreached people group.
- The church's mission giving is targeted primarily, although not exclusively, on the chosen unreached people group.
- Once the focus on the one people group is well established, there might come a time when the church is ready to add another people group to its global involvement.

Why Is It Valuable for a Church to Have a Focused Approach to Mission?

It allows the fellowship to understand the mission. Picture the scene of what Sunday morning is like for many Christians. They hurry to church, negotiate a parking place, get the kids to their places, and slip into a seat in the worship center just as the service starts. As the service is ending, their minds race to review how they are going to pick up the kids, see the people they need to see, get home, get lunch, and get everybody ready for the demanding week in front of them.

We come to the subject of mission from harried, crowded lives that offer us little mental or emotional space. How are we going to meaningfully track the ten, twenty, or thirty missionaries, countries, or mission projects our church may be financially supporting? It is all a maze and not something screaming loudly enough to cause us to take the time and energy to connect with it.

I have been speaking on mission in churches for over thirty-five years and listening to the questions people ask afterwards. They are genuinely well intentioned. But generally folks have little grasp on what is going on with the missionaries and mission projects their church supports. They don't have enough information and perspective to understand. How could they?

Churches focused on one to two unreached people groups generally stand in sharp contrast. For members of the congregation, the identity of the chosen people group has worked its way to the front of their minds. The missions information they receive at church is in-depth, substantive, and satisfying. As they watch the news, or in their own reading, their minds collect, process, and integrate information that comes to them about this people.

They, their friends, or their children may soon serve on a short-term mission trip to this people. As others from the fellowship go as cross-cultural witnesses to the same group, some of their friends may be among them. After several years of hearing about the church's initiative among this people, praying for it, learning about it, and being connected with others involved in it, mission moves to a place of meaningful involvement in a person's life.

> *After several years of hearing about the church's initiative among this people, praying for it, learning about it, and being connected with others involved in it, mission moves to a place of meaningful involvement in a person's life.*

It allows the fellowship to own the mission. What is our first response when faced with the decision as to whether we want to buy or own something? We want to know about it. If it is a car, we might research the repair record of the make and model. If it is a house, we will want to know about the neighborhood, the builder, nearby schools and shopping, and any previous problems.

The more we can research and think about a decision, the more comfortable we get with the final outcome. The more people can hear about their church's decision to focus on an unreached people group, the more information and perspective they can gain, the more they can think and pray about it, the more likely it is that they will own it from their hearts.

It allows the fellowship to participate in the mission. Once we own something from our hearts, we will want to invest in it. In the next chapter there is a fuller description of church fellowships participating in mission.

It provides a context in which missionaries (cross-cultural ministers) can receive the best possible support. The fellowship understands the mission of those who minister cross-culturally and shares ownership of that mission with them. Those who serve overseas can spend more time with the church fellowship when they are home. Relationships and friendships can be developed in depth. People from the fellowship serving on short-term outreaches

> *A deepened understanding of the mission and personal relationships increase the capacity of the fellowship to pray, to offer pastoral care to missionaries, and to ensure financial support.*

and coaching visits can deepen these relationships. A deepened understanding of the mission and personal relationships increase the capacity of the fellowship to pray, to offer pastoral care to missionaries, and to ensure financial support.

Questions People Ask about a Focused Approach to Mission

If our church moves in this direction will we have to stop supporting all the missionaries we are now supporting? Absolutely not. Begin to move toward this approach by seeking the Lord about the people group he may be leading you to strategically engage. Examine closely where the missionaries you currently support are now serving. Is there a people group represented among them whom God may be leading you to select?

Next, stop taking on new missionaries for support, at least temporarily. Give yourself permission to begin to build a "war chest"—funds held in reserve for the strategic kingdom initiative being birthed among you. Wait for the people group to emerge that God has for you. Be open for God to bring to you new missionaries who are already called to the group God has for you.

Recognize that attrition affects almost every church's roster of missionaries. As folks do not return to the field for whatever reason, do not feel compelled to add a replacement right away. Add more funds to the war chest.

Once the group is chosen, many churches find that they want to keep supporting missionaries serving elsewhere with whom they have meaningful, long-term relationships.

What if God is leading our church to support a number of missionaries? Choosing one people group feels too much like man's planning rather than being led by the Spirit. This kind of focused approach is *not* for every church. By all means, follow your own sense of God's direction for your fellowship. There are many churches with a very effective global outreach that have not been led in a focused approach.

Remember too that a majority of churches are smaller rather than larger, and a focused approach might work especially well for them. But there are no rules here, except to be led by the Lord into the approach he has for you.

A church definitely needs to be led by the Spirit if it is to choose a people group. This decision needs to come out of a context of extended, focused prayer for God's direction. The fellowship and the leaders need to have a clear sense of God's direction and calling.

As a missionary, what if I want a particular church to support me but am called to a people group they have not chosen to focus on? Consider putting together before the Lord a group of churches who would embrace the people group you have been called to. Any church that selects a group will need to network and partner with others. For God to use you to catalyze such a network might produce beautiful kingdom fruit for the people group, for the churches involved, and for your personal ministry. As you seek God about this, ask him to give you churches in roughly the same locality. You don't want to be like my friends who had to drive from Maine to southern California to connect with their sending constituency!

What Is a Strategic Approach to Missions?

A strategic approach to missions is

- to make a proactive choice,
- to understand the overall remaining task in world mission,

- to identify the portion of this task which has been completed, and
- to invest oneself in the portion of the task remaining.

I once met a young man from the United States who was going to be a missionary in a country in northern Europe. I was saddened. I knew the situation in that country. I had friends who were from this country, and I had spoken in a number of churches there. The country enjoys a rich spiritual heritage. Prayer and revival movements over the last two hundred years have been strong. The Church in this country has exhibited a commitment to world evangelization that has been exemplary. Based on its population, it is probably one of the top missionary sending countries in the world! A person would be hard pressed to present the decision to go to that country as a missionary as being strategic in any sense of the word.

I asked this young man how he chose that country. He replied, "When I was in Bible school, a missionary from that country came to speak to us in chapel. He gave us each a coin from the country and asked us to use the coin to remind us to pray. I prayed for the country, and God called me there."

When someone says, "God called me there," it tends to shut down any further conversation about whether such a decision is wise or responsible or grounded in present realities. God has called, end of conversation.

> When someone says, "God called me there," it shuts down any further conversation about whether such a decision is wise or responsible or grounded in present realities.

I certainly do not want to be judgmental or unkind. But one thing is clear: the missionary force is terribly unevenly deployed throughout the earth. Ninety percent are serving in areas like this particular country where the church has already been established.

Only 10 percent are found ministering among nations who have yet to be discipled. Is this God's doing?

Is God really sending only 10 percent of the missionary force to the unreached world? Or is this situation a symptom of our being poorly informed? Or of our habits of making subjective decisions based on personal preference and what is easier? Or of us not hearing correctly what God is really saying?

A strategic approach to missions says, "We want to invest responsibly with the end goal in mind. We want to be intentional. We want to know what we are doing and why we are doing it."

A Strategic Approach to Missions

A local church pastor recently said something to me that I found incredibly insightful but troubling. "In war," he said, "the generals make the decisions, not the privates. When faced with the decision to send tens of thousands of soldiers to the beaches of Normandy in June 1944, General Eisenhower did not ask the privates where they wanted to go. If he had, they probably would have chosen North Africa where the victory had already been won. It would have been much easier! No, in war, the generals take responsibility for making the decisions, and they base their decisions on the strategic imperatives that confront them."

The pastor continued, "In missions, we have grown accustomed to allowing the privates to make the decisions, even though they often decide to go to places where the missiological victory has already been won."

In a strategic approach to missions, we make intentional decisions to deploy personnel and invest resources according to the biblical imperative presented to us: "*All peoples on earth shall be blessed!*" Having sought the Lord with all our hearts, with his last instructions clearly before us, and based on the best information available, we resolutely press forward toward the goal of completing the task Jesus entrusted to us—all of us.

In five years, coaching churches in strategically focused missions will be a growth industry. Will Antioch Network be ready?
—Mission leader

After I had finished my talk "Local Churches Starting New Churches among Unreached Peoples," a woman sitting in the back of the room raised her hand. "Can you give us specifics as to how a church would go about doing this?" she asked.

I smiled to myself. A common critique when I speak on this subject is that some people find my words are long on vision and short on application. This time I had come prepared. I had what seemed to me to be fairly well developed specifics describing the path a church would follow.

When I finished my extended, thought-out answer, she raised her hand again. "Can you give us specifics as to how a church would go about doing this?"

Chapter 19

The Stages[15]

Actually there are a variety of ways to answer this woman's question. There is no precise recipe. Each church's journey will be delightfully unique. We stand near the front end of knowledge that is being discovered by a blend of different churches. There are no experts here, no definitive, final answers. Each church's journey and discoveries add to our knowledge base. Nevertheless, the movement has begun. The pioneers have left the starting point and have blazed a trail far enough to offer valuable perspective and guidance to those who will be the next to embark.

For years churches have asked Antioch Network to define the process. These stages represent our best effort to date. They are our distillation of what churches have taught us. They are not presented as a final statement but the latest draft. They must be evaluated by each church as it gains its own experience and be subject to continual revision as new knowledge is discovered.

Let's frame this discussion in two broad sections. First, it might be helpful to overview some characteristics one tends to find in the churches that are birthing initiatives to start churches among an unreached people group. Then, we will want to explore what the process might look like.

Church Characteristics

What might be some common characteristics in a fellowship whom the Holy Spirit is preparing to launch an initiative among an unreached people group and possibly start new churches? We do not mean to imply that all of these must be fully developed before a church can begin down this road. Not at all! In fact, a focus on pioneer church planting has, in many cases, helped to strengthen or even birth some of these characteristics within a congregation.

Vital public worship. Biblical corporate worship has its focus on God—to declare his glory, to love him, and to minister to him. It also has a profound effect on the worshippers. It sparks vision. It fuels faith. It brings healing. It is a powerful form of spiritual warfare. These things prepare a body of believers for world mission.

Leadership with a vision beyond the church. People follow vision, especially vision that is God given and God empowered. Godly leaders do not impose their vision on the church. They hear God's call to the body, declare that call with authority, and lovingly cultivate a response of obedience.

A high view of the local church. When we see the church as God designed it to be, we see "the fullness of him who fills everything in every way" (Eph. 1:23). Jesus is present in the church, expressing his love for the world to the church and through it. The Holy Spirit is present, releasing the gifts he has given for ministry. The community of faith is God the Father's agent for personal salvation, social reformation, and kingdom extension.

Committed corporate and private prayer. As individual believers and churches mature, they become increasingly aware of the ongoing counter-attack by the enemy of God on the church. A commitment to kingdom extension, especially among the unreached, will be derailed quickly without a corresponding commitment to spiritual warfare. Prayer must be central.

Powerful small groups. It is in small groups that nurture and life transformation take place. Powerful mission flows from those who have drunk deeply of the redemptive life of Christ. Small groups form the framework for leadership development throughout a church. The gifts and calling of tomorrow's church planters can be recognized and developed as they lead small groups.

Leadership development. God has designed reproduction as a fundamental function of healthy life. The more a church is filled with God's life, the more it will experience the instinct to reproduce. The same is true of God's leaders. As mature church leaders invest themselves in the younger leaders God entrusts to them, a new generation of church planters will emerge.

A mindset for partnership. Powerful churches, increasingly aware of the God-given capacity they carry, are also in touch with the areas where they are incomplete. No church has it all. Filled with a God-generated humility, they desire to express unity with the wider body of Christ in tangible ways. This sets the stage for beautiful partnerships to occur with other churches and mission organizations.

Apostolic structures. The empowerment to start churches among unreached peoples is apostolic in nature, and apostolic ministry calls for apostolic structures. Some churches have created their own organizations for the purpose of kingdom extension that are rooted in and express the life of the fellowship. Others have formed mutually supportive partnerships with mission organizations. In this case, the mission organization serves as the apostolic structure through which the church expresses its calling. A third option is some hybrid of these two.

A growing passion to reproduce. As churches experience the power of Jesus living among them and see the potential of Christian community to change societies, the passion for birthing new churches in unreached cultures grows. They long for the glory of God to be proclaimed where it is least known, and they see God raising up new apostolic leaders among them.

Stages a Church Goes through to Engage a People Group

There will be unique features in each church's journey. These stages represent the current understanding of people who are being taught by the churches we work with. If your church's process doesn't fit this framework, by all means lay aside the framework!

The sequential progression of these stages is inexact. There is a sense in which envisioning comes before training. But sometimes during a prayer journey for the purpose of envisioning, the stages of strategizing and training may begin. The overall process must be living and God directed. Generally, once a stage has begun, it is ongoing. Envisioning is never complete. The process of committing will be challenged regularly and probably need to go deeper. Strategizing will require ongoing adjustments based upon the experience gained. And when is the training of a servant of God ever complete?

These stages can serve as a framework, a road map, or a benchmark. They are offered as a practical help to churches as they move forward in their call to proclaim his grace among the nations.

Stage One: Envisioning Your Church

During this stage, the vision for church planting among an unreached people is proclaimed, taught, and nurtured within the fellowship. This is done by church leaders and those they invite to address and to work with the fellowship. It is made clear that the church is beginning a different way of looking at mission. It is not just sending missionaries. It is sending its own people—friends and family from the congregation. Leadership is moving toward the goal of the whole church owning the mission. The fellowship will explore the reasoning behind this strategic approach to mission and grow in their passion to reach the lost and their conviction that this is the strategy God is calling them to embrace.

Any member of the congregation can be the catalyst that begins the envisioning process, but until the senior leaders have embraced the vision, it is the proposal of a group of individuals rather than the process of a church. An important milestone is for the fellowship to reach the place where it can embrace a focused approach to missions, concentrating its resources—giftings, energies, and finances—to reach a strategically selected people group. There are a few important components of stage one:

Prayer. The church enters a season of seeking God for his will in this matter. It will be crucial for the congregation to have a sense that it has heard from the Lord. For example, the Moravians of the eighteenth century sent out more missionaries than all Protestants before them put together. They established a twenty-four-hour prayer chain that lasted one hundred years.

Mission education. The church seeks to understand God's overall mission on earth studying biblical material, the history of missions, and the progress of world evangelization. What is God's mission on earth? What part can be considered completed? What is remaining to be done? For many churches, the process either began or was bolstered through enrolling many of their members in the Perspectives Course, a general mission course that looks at God's mission through biblical, historical, cultural, and strategic perspectives.

Exploratory trips among unreached peoples. Through these exploratory trips, the church gains valuable firsthand information and enters a prime place from which to seek God's direction and confirmation in prayer. Northside Community Church in Atlanta, Georgia, sent over one-third of their fellowship on short-term ministry trips to Bosnia. No wonder the church was filled with vision and love for these people.

Stage Two: Committing to a People Group

This stage involves processing the information and experiences that took place during the envisioning stage so the church can make a decision about adopting a specific unreached people group. During the envisioning stage, the church has embraced a philosophy of strategic focus and has had direct exposure to unreached peoples. Now it is time to narrow the possibilities and discern which particular people group God is calling the church to engage. There are some conditions important to stage two:

The senior leadership must be committed to the mission. They must sense that this is part of God's call upon the church. It is not enough for them to passively endorse what others want to do.

There needs to be a growing sense of ownership throughout the body. This new, strategic approach to missions will be a fruit of the envisioning ministry of the church's leaders.

The church needs to count the cost. The church's leaders must be willingly dependant upon the Lord and trust him for whatever the mission requires. The elders of Trinity Church in Omaha, Nebraska, have recommitted themselves to their adopted people group twice as they have grown in their understanding of the cost involved in reaching them.

Stage Three: Strategizing the Approach

This stage involves developing a strategy for reaching the selected people group. The resources and gifting of the church must be considered along with the unique opportunities and challenges of the people group. The possibility of partnering with other churches and mission organizations comes into play at this point. The goal is to develop a plan that gets the church moving in the right direction although there will be additions and deletions along the way. The primary question in this stage is "How do we implement our decision to adopt this particular people group?" There are other important questions to ask while pursing stage three.

What are the opportunities among our target people group? What are their real and felt needs? Medical? Educational? Business skills? Language skills? How do we place our people among them? Do some individuals and families from our adopted people group live in our home city? Might we begin ministering among them here? Open Door Fellowship in Phoenix, Arizona, initiated an extensive outreach among local Bosnian refugees as a foundation for subsequent church planting in Bosnia.

What are the strengths of our church? What spiritual gifts are our people strong in? What areas of vocational expertise are prevalent among us? How has God led us as a church up to now? How might that experience come into play in reaching our unreached people group? Union Chapel in Muncie, Indiana, took up medical work among the Kazaks because the needs among them were great and their team was blessed with a number of medical professionals.

What are the threats to this mission? What might derail us among our adopted people? Political realities? Economic vulnerabilities? Among us as a church? Where might the enemy's attacks most likely be directed?

In what areas might our church need help from others? Whom might we access for that help? What connections with the larger body of Christ do we already enjoy? Other churches? Organizations? Mission agencies? What kinds of partnerships are we going to need? The International Turkey Network, made up of churches, agencies, and individuals, was formed largely through the initiatives of churches aware of their need to partner with a community focused on Turkey.

Stage Four: Training the Participants

This stage involves the identification, training, and release of personnel capable of implementing the strategic plan. One might assume that we are talking exclusively about field personnel. No. Training and equipping those central to the initiative but who will remain at home is vitally important. This is an on-going process that spans the life of the initiative and is connected to its overall success. The fact that God loves to use "ordinary people" and that every believer can play a significant role in world evangelization must never give us permission to minimize thorough and effective training in every area. In stage four, there are specific areas where training is needed:

Spiritual-life formation. Serving among an unreached people will test individuals' personal maturity and character. It will not be enough to be a missions enthusiast. The formation of an inner life like Jesus is not something that just comes upon us. It must be learned through discipleship to him. Does the church have a process of teaching members discipleship to Jesus?

Leaders and congregational members based in the sending church. A person who will coordinate the overall support operation must be trained. A strong administrative team must be equipped. The congregation must be taught how to participate in the effort through group prayer. Pastorally gifted members must be trained to minister to those who go.

Team life. The initiative will inevitably require us to work with others in pressure situations. Personal issues will surface that might be undetected in normal life at home. Wholeness and maturity in interpersonal relationships must be tested, developed, and proven. Dynamics of team life and ministry must be taught.

Cross-cultural ministry. Ministering in another culture requires some significantly different understandings from ministering at home. For those who go, understanding principles involved in cross-cultural ministry is a must.

Church planting. Seek practical insights from experienced church planters. What has caused their successes, their failures? A study of materials on church planting selected by those going to the field and key church leaders should be a top priority. Creating or finding opportunities for those being sent to gain experience in church planting at home can enhance effectiveness significantly. Immanuel Fellowship of Frisco, Colorado, has as its central goal in mission involvement to be the home base for a training institute for church planters in a local church setting.

Stage Five: Engaging the People Group

This stage begins with the establishment of an effective ministry among the chosen people group, and it continues until they are reached or until God leads the church to disengage. The challenge during this stage is maintaining focus and commitment over long periods of time when there may be few tangible results to report. Church planting among unreached peoples is often a long and challenging process. There are five potential forms of engagement in stage five:

1. The church can send its own church planting team, facilitated through an apostolic organizational structure formed by the church. Ichthus Fellowship in London, England, sent a team to Istanbul, Turkey, where a Turkish church has now been turned over to Turkish leadership.

2. The church can send a church planting team in partnership with a mission organization. Grace Fellowship Church in Baltimore, Maryland, has worked in partnership with a mission agency in sending their first team to an unreached people group in Asia.

3. The church can send some of its members as part of another church planting team in partnership with another church or mission agency.

4. The church can render practical support to a church planting initiative already underway among the adopted people.

5. The church can provide assistance to the emerging national church among the adopted people as it seeks to reproduce. The Evangelical Church of Mostar, Bosnia, is now reproducing itself among the peoples of Bosnia through the mentoring it has received from Northside Community Church of Atlanta, Georgia.

Post-Engagement Issues to Keep in Mind

Additional personnel will probably be needed both on the field and at home. Over time, it is likely that some original team members will need to return home from the field. And as the initiative matures, different gifts and skill sets may be needed on the field and at home. The training process can be ongoing, with new team members continually being prepared.

New partnerships can be forged. Sometimes the most powerful partnerships are those begun while informally working together on the field. That which begins and grows naturally and informally can be recognized and formalized.

Pastoral care for long-term field personnel is critical. Living and ministering among an unreached people for months and years is very demanding spiritually, emotionally, and physically. The strains on family life are intense. Healthy churches are filled with pastorally gifted and experienced people who can be employed in the long-term care of those who go. Developing the capacity to deliver that care and sustain it over the long haul highlights the level of commitment required on the part of the whole church, both leaders and people.

The Fruit

I have just read a report from a church planting team who is serving among one of the unreached people groups in former Soviet Central Asia. They were sent out by a church in Indiana, which has now been joined by churches in Virginia and Oregon. Two of the churches are denominational (different denominations), and one is an independent church. The team has been in a village, located along the ancient Silk Road, for five years. When they arrived in the village, there were no believers there. Today their gatherings number more than twenty believers, and momentum is growing. To God be the glory, great things he has done!

We need a movement of churches like these three!

---

[15]The booklet "Stages," by George Miley and Steve Unangst, published by Antioch Network, provided the basis for this chapter.

A call for an international movement, focused on the completion of world evangelization, rooted in and coming forth from local churches.

More than one observer has commented that local churches, in too many cases, lack vision beyond themselves and their own interests. But the only person qualified to make such an assessment is Jesus. In cases where this is indeed his evaluation, his specially chosen and prepared messengers must be the ones who deliver it. It must never come in a critical spirit. None of us has permission to stand in the place of critic of Christ's church.

Christ's message will come to the church as a word of grace as well as a word of truth and of call. And if it comes, it must be heard and received, for it is indeed a serious message. The only appropriate response is repentance. It would indicate that, in some crucial ways, the church has been formed more by the world than by the Lord. Jesus is not self-absorbed.

Senior pastors and church leaders, what is the Spirit saying to the churches? What do you hear?

CHAPTER 20

A Movement

"Everything must be fulfilled that is written about me in the Law of Moses, the Prophets and the Psalms. . . . This is what is written: The Christ will suffer and rise from the dead on the third day, and repentance and forgiveness of sins will be preached in his name to all nations" (Luke 24:44; 46–47).

What directions is Jesus giving us today as to how we are to go about finishing his directions to us 2,000 years ago? We have approximately 6,600 nations or people groups to go. If that sounds like a lot, remember there are 600 churches in the world for every one unreached people group.

We have discussed the benefits of a local church adopting a strategic focused approach to missions and concentrated on activities aimed at church planting among one unreached people group. Can one church bless a nation all on its own? No! Other churches and mission organizations will need to join in.

How many churches will this take? It is hard to say. Much depends on the size of the people group, the political, social, and economic conditions among them and the capacity of the churches involved. But remember, there are 600 churches in the world for every one unreached people group.

For the sake of having a starting point, let's say, on average, we need a network of five churches together with some mission organizations to bless one people group. Remember, there are 600 churches in the world for every one unreached people group.

This task is doable. If that conviction could only permeate our hearts, our plans, and our priorities. This task is *doable*!

What if five churches were to choose unreached people group #1 as their focus? And what if, while they were working on how they were going to bless that people group, another five churches were to choose unreached people group #2 as their focus? And what if, while they were working on how they were going to reach that people group, another five churches were to choose unreached people group #3 as their focus? And what if, while they were working on how they were going to start churches among that people group, ...and on and on.

What if more churches began to hear about what was going on? "Wow, look at this," they might say to each other. "There are churches that are meaningfully, strategically, and effectively connecting with God's global purposes and making a difference! Wonder if we could be part of that?"

What if the churches that were engaging unreached people groups would say to these other churches, "If you would like, we will help you. When we started, we did not feel like we knew very much about what we were doing. It was the Lord who taught us. We would be happy to share our experiences, failures, and successes with you. We would be honored to coach and encourage you"?

What if, while this kind of phenomenon was taking place in one country where there are lots and lots of churches, the same kind of thing began to happen in another country where there are lots and lots of churches, and then in another...and another, etc.? There are scores of countries in the world in which there are plenty of churches that could do this.

That could start a grassroots movement, rooted in and coming forth from local churches, focused on completing world evangelization. Remember, there are 600 churches in the world for every one unreached people group.

What Might Such a Movement of Churches Look Like?

In seeking to picture what such a grassroots movement might look like, we are forced to go beyond giving examples of what has already happened. In my understanding, we are calling for something that has never happened before. I know of no examples! Throughout *Loving the Church...Blessing the Nations,* I have tried very hard not to be just theoretical. We have sought time after time to give real-life, historical examples of what we have been talking about. This was especially true of the last chapter, but certainly not only there.

Once all is said and done, every concrete example in this book is merely a lower-level component of what I am calling for here. I, along with Antioch Network, am calling for a higher-level, broad-based movement, international in scope, that will sweep the body of Christ across the finish line and bring about the completion of the marathon of world mission that has been going on for centuries. *Does anybody want to finish this thing?*

So, in conceptualizing this movement, we must gather our best creative powers of imagination and projection and project into a preferred future. What might such a movement look like?

It would be grassroots, bottom-up, decentralized. It would not be controlled by any organization, denomination, or network, although denominations and church networks would certainly take part, along with mission organizations. There would be the feeling that each denomination, network, church, and organization was esteeming the others better than themselves.

It would be energized by vision. Jesus must be worshipped, loved, and obeyed among *all* nations on earth. Nothing else honors him. Nothing less is acceptable.

It would be highly relational. Godly relationships between churches, mission organizations, and their leaders, would allow prayer, information, experience, training, technology, personnel, and even funding to flow freely across church and organizational borders. There would be a pervasive feeling that it was an initiative of the kingdom of God.

It would be led by church leaders. A network or movement of churches is, in a fundamental sense, a network or movement of church leaders. God must raise up a generation of church leaders who will lead people into battle among the nations. The role of apostolic leaders in this apostolic-type movement would be recognized and celebrated. Pastors and apostolic leaders would beautifully honor one another.

It would be international. Churches and church leaders from Latin America, Africa, and Asia would participate fully with their brethren from Europe and North America. More and more, it could be expected to see them giving leadership to the movement.

It would partner with mission organizations. As churches began to move, they would quickly realize the rich heritage and experience mission organizations offer. Relationships would develop between churches and mission organizations that allowed both to offer their strengths to the other. They would serve together in ways that fully honored their Lord and one another.

Loving the Church...Blessing the Nations is a call for this movement—*an international movement, focused on the completion of world evangelization, rooted in and coming forth from local churches.*

Antioch Network

It is the vision of such a movement that has been the daily motivation of members of Antioch Network since the first meeting of seven churches on March 16, 1987.

What we are talking about here, of course, is and must be much wider and broader and deeper than what is known as Antioch Network. But we are available to Jesus and his church to serve this movement in whatever ways we are able—as servant, champion, facilitator, coach, resource, or friend.

How can we serve you?

For more information contact:

Antioch Network
5060 North 19th Avenue, Suite 306
Phoenix, AZ 85015
USA
Phone: (602) 589-7777
E-mail: info@antiochnetwork.org
Website: www.antiochnetwork.org